A gift to Bill from Jake Grabow, owner of Gold's Gym in Ashland, Oregon. Artwork by Michael Arciniega, www.marciniega.com.

This page has been intentionally left blank.

BEYOND THE

THE BILL PEARL STORY

UNIVERSE

REVISED EDITION

BILL PEARL

WITH KIM SHOTT

Beyond the Universe

The Bill Pearl Story

Revised Edition

Written by Bill Pearl with Kim Shott
Published by Bill Pearl
Edited by George and Tuesday Coates
Cover design and layout by Richard R Thornley Jr

Bill Pearl
P.O. Box 1080
Phoenix, Oregon 97535
Email: support@billpearl.com
Website: www.billpearl.com

ISBN-13 for Revised Soft Cover edition: 978-1-938855-23-8

NOTICE OF RIGHTS

DEDICATION

I dedicate this book to my wife, Judy. Through her love and support I have been able to obtain a higher state of self-fulfillment.

Bill Pearl

ACKNOWLEDGMENTS

In compiling this book, *Beyond the Universe*, it was necessary to secure information from several sources other than my own memory. I have, therefore, quoted and used several outlets for material. Many people have given time, advice, information, encouragement, help and allowed me the use of their photographs and publications to compile and complete this project.

I would like to thank all of them and a small portion by name in alphabetical order: Mike Arciniega, Bob Autry, Joanne Autry, Jennifer Brown, Lloyd Kahn, Kathi Hilmes, Raymond Long, Jake Grabow, Jim Mess, Jim Morris, Gene Mozee, Judy Pearl, Bob Rogers, Kim Shott, Max Shott, Brandie Thornley, Jacob Thornley, Richard Thornley, Kimberly Pearl Wyniarczuk, Roman Wyniarczuk, David Young and Harold Zinkin.

From among the many thousands of loyal fans who have been helpful to me in my career of weight training and the close friendships I have acquired, I would particularly like to thank Leo Stern.

* * * * * *

Co-author, Kim Shott, would first and foremost like to thank Bill and Judy Pearl for an opportunity of a lifetime. Kim would also like to thank those who have directly and indirectly contributed to the creation of *Beyond the Universe* including, but not limited to: Lawson Inada and Sandra Holstein for their guidance and inspiration, Dr. Bill Gholson for his editorial style and rhetorical skill, and both Ellen Cullmer and Karen Kendrick, whose invaluable transcription of taped interviews led to the seven-hundred-fifty-page foundation of this book. Finally, Kim would like to thank Max, Eli and Sam Shott for their unwavering support and encouragement.

Kim and her husband, Max, own and operate an orthopedic and sports physical therapy clinic in Ashland, Oregon.

Bill and Leo Stern in 1961 with Stonehenge in the background.

Left: The symmetry of Pearl's physique gave a statue-like quality to many of his poses and people often underestimated his size and weight.

TITLES AND AWARDS

1952 Mr. San Diego, 3rd place (San Diego, California)

1952 Mr. Oceanside (Oceanside, California)

1953 Mr. Southern California (Los Angeles, California)

1953 Mr. California (Los Angeles, California)

1953 AAU Mr. America (Indianapolis, Indiana)

1953 NABBA Mr. Universe, Amateur (London, England)

1956 Mr. USA, Professional (Los Angeles, California)

1956 NABBA Mr. Universe, Professional, Tall Man's Class (London, England)

1961 NABBA Mr. Universe, Professional (London, England)

1967 NABBA Mr. Universe, Professional (London, England)

1971 NABBA Mr. Universe, Professional (London, England)

1974 WBBA World's Best-Built Man of the Century (New York)

1978 Entered into WBBA Hall of Fame (New York, New York)

1978 Elected the IFBB National Chairman of the Professional Physique Judges Committee (Acapulco, Mexico)

1988 Entered into Pioneers of Fitness Hall of Fame

1992 Entered into Gold's Gym Hall of Fame

1994 Guest of Honor of the Association of Oldetime Barbell & Strongmen 12th Annual Reunion

1994 Entered into The Joe Weider Hall of Fame

1995 AAU Lifetime Achievement Award

1996 American Powerlifters Federation Hall of Fame

1997 International Chiropractors Association Sports & Fitness Man of the Year

2000 Spirit of Muscle Beach Award

2001 World Gym Lifetime Achievement Award

2001 Society of Weight-Training Injury Specialists Lifetime Achievement Award

2002 Canadian Fitness Award for 60+ Years of Inspiration to the Industry

2002 National Fitness Trade Journal Lifetime Achievement Award

2003 *Iron Man Magazine* Peary & Mabel Rader Lifetime Achievement Award

2004 Arnold Schwarzenegger Lifetime Achievement Award

2006 Pro Division Inc. Lifetime Achievement Award

2010 National Fitness Hall of Fame Lifetime Achievement Award

2011 Natural Bodybuilding Lifetime Achievement Award

Bill Pearl's competitive bodybuilding career spanned a term of nearly twenty years, which is the longest any top physique star has ever endured. During his entire career of competitive bodybuilding, Bill competed in the short sum of eleven physique contests, which is less than some physique men will compete in during a single year. With these eleven contests, Bill won every top physique title there was to win and some titles several times. Pearl's motto is "Strive for quality rather than for quantity."

INTRODUCTION

Most people dream, some aspire and a few succeed. Even after all the years I'd spent in school I never learned to harness my own aspiration for success. I assumed there were those destined for great things leaving the rest of us destined to be in awe of them. It wasn't until years after I'd made a phone call to one of bodybuilding's legends that I'd come to understand there really is a hero in us all.

Helen Keller once wrote, "No pessimist ever discovered the secrets of the stars or sailed to an uncharted land, or showed a new way for the human spirit." Yet, whether it's the society we live in or human nature, realizing a dream is often met with pessimism. In my case, whether it was starting college at the age of sixteen, living in New Zealand coaching softball, or working with Bill on this book, I knew deep down that I couldn't fail achieving goals I wanted so badly.

By the time I met Mr. Bill Pearl I'd matured past my youthful arrogance when I thought I'd take the world by the horns to the stage where I realized the world had much bigger horns than I'd bargained for. Still, I went to Mr. Pearl's office with a stomach full of nerves and a briefcase containing a list of publications, including only one short story and a poem, that served merely to show I was extremely wet behind the ears with regard to my writing career.

It's been five years since we started collaboration on *Beyond the Universe* and I'll never forget the first meeting we had. Bill said to me, as he offered his hand, "So we're both in this to the end--for the good of it or bad?" I took his hand, gladly, without having a clue how difficult and at times frustrating, but overwhelmingly satisfying the journey I was embarking on was to be. I finally learned what makes a champion.

A champion has to always push harder than they think they can. A champion has to have a fire in his or her belly no one can squelch. A champion has to believe their dream will be realized so that when their break comes they don't hesitate, they don't squander it, they take it by the horns and ride it for all it's glory until the bitter end of victory.

Kim Shott

Photograph of Pearl taken by Leo Stern just prior to competing in the 1971 Professional NABBA Mr. Universe contest. Pearl's body weight was 242 pounds.

CONTENTS

Chapter I

LESSONS

A Bag of Tools
Isn't it strange that princes and kings
And clowns that caper in sawdust rings
And just plain folks like you and me
Are builders for eternity?

To each is given a bag of tools,
A shapeless mass and book of rules,
And each must build, ere life has flown,
A stumbling block or steppingstone.

R. L. Sharpe

"What in the hell am I doing up here! I've been standing at attention for over an hour! The judges have us turning every which way but loose. The only thing that they haven't had us do is to turn our backs to the audience, drop our posing briefs and show the cracks of our ass. Enough is enough! When am I going to learn? Forty-one years old and still letting others control my life! You would think I'd have learned something competing in these contests over the past 18 years and I have. Nothing has changed; nothing is going to change when it comes to judging physique contests."

Those were a few of the thoughts running through

Bill waving to the audience as Chris Dickerson, 1970 AAU Mr. America (far right), happily smiles and claps to show approval.

my mind while standing onstage at the Victoria Palace in London, England, on Friday, September 17, 1971, for the prejudging of the Amateur and Professional NABBA Mr. Universe contests. The show was billed, "The Physique Contest of The Century." Virtually every top bodybuilder in the world was competing, except Arnold Schwarzenegger, the reigning champion for the past three years.

Joe Weider and Arnold Schwarzenegger had goaded me into entering the contest. Weider began by publishing articles in his fitness magazines asserting that I was afraid to compete against the current crop of bodybuilders. Arnold chimed in with similar remarks. I could understand Arnold's desire to compete against me. It made sense that he wanted my name added to his list. I was one of the few top bodybuilders he hadn't defeated.

In truth, if Leo Stern, my coach and dear friend, hadn't talked me into it, I wouldn't have entered. I had retired from competition after winning the 1967 NABBA Professional Mr. Universe title. I couldn't have cared less about what Joe or Arnold had to say. However, Leo took their snide remarks more personally. With every phone call it was, "Why are you letting these guys take shots at you? Get off your dead-ass and do something about it!" With that in mind, I made it known in all major physique magazines that Bill Pearl would compete in the 1971 NABBA Professional Mr. Universe contest. This would

Left: Possibly in the best condition of his life, at the age of 41, this photograph was taken of Pearl immediately after winning the 1971 NABBA Professional Mr. Universe crown in London, England.

Bill reaching to shake Arnold Schwarzenegger's hand for winning the 1967 NABBA Amateur Mr. Universe title.

definitely be the last chance for everyone to have a crack at me.

That time had come. Standing onstage being compared to Sergio Oliva, Frank Zane, Reg Park, Tony Emmott, Kassem Yazbek, Roy Duval, Chris Dickerson and approximately one hundred twenty other great physiques from around the world, the audience murmured, "Where's Arnold?"

Why hadn't he competed? It was obvious he was in top physical condition. The following weekend he entered

Arnold Schwarzenegger and Joe Weider congratulate Bill when he was inducted into the Pioneers of Fitness Hall of Fame, in 1988.

and won his second IFBB Mr. Olympia title in Paris, France. If my memory serves, only two contestants vied for the title.

What I know for certain is that a few weeks prior to the NABBA Mr. Universe contest, Leo and I attended a warm-up posing exhibition given by Arnold in Santa Monica, California. Weider approached Leo to say, "What do you think?" Leo replied, "Arnold's in great shape." Weider went on, "He's going to compete in the NABBA Mr. Universe in a couple of weeks." Leo replied, "Pearl's going to rip him a new one."

Weider and Stern had known each other since the mid 1940s. It may have been that Joe's respect for Leo's judgment of physiques caused him to realize that Leo was serious with his comment. Possibly Weider decided it was too much of a risk to take the chance of Arnold's being beaten in a physique contest by someone nearly old enough to be his father. At that time, Arnold was under contract to Weider. His magazine touted him as "The World's Greatest Bodybuilder." Nearly every issue featured training articles, supposedly written by Arnold, along with endorsements for everything Weider sold. In retrospect, I believe Arnold would have competed if the decision had been left to him. He was one of the fiercest competitors I've seen on stage. His motto should have been, "Win at all cost." With all due respect, several years later, Arnold apologized for making the 1971 NABBA Mr. Universe challenge. He commented that he understood the burden he had placed on me at that stage of *my* life because he had reached that stage of *his* life.

To make the prejudging more interesting for the audience that year, one of the major competitors was so obviously bombed out of his head, he was having difficulty responding to the judges' instructions. Sergio Oliva helped the entertainment by standing in the line-up loudly complaining that he was hungry, as his two-hour pump-up was causing him to deflate like a slow leak in the Hindenburg. To further add to the audience's delight, Reg Park, a previous three-time winner, kept up a running word battle with Oliva on how bad each of them thought the other looked. My main concern was getting offstage. After standing in a flexed position for over an hour, my calves had cramped so badly I wasn't sure I could move. The cramping began during the comparison portion of the prejudging and we still had the overall posing and final comparisons to go through.

Before competition began, an incident occurred that might have had a slight difference in the outcome of the

Sergio Oliva onstage at the 1971 NABBA Professional Mr. Universe contest.

winner of the NABBA Amateur Mr. Universe, the year before, was obviously upset. He verbally showed it by claiming that the two of us hadn't been properly compared, side-by-side. Sergio Oliva hadn't let up, not because he was still hungry, but because he wouldn't receive the $5,000.00 bonus promised to him by Arthur Jones, of Nautilus Gym Equipment, if he had won the contest. Reg Park was still slightly vocal commenting on the judging, saying something like, "Where did they find these guys?" Chris Dickerson, winner of the 1970 AAU Mr. America title, remained a gentleman by standing in the background smiling at everyone without a bad word to say. He seemed to take my victory in stride.

I had coached Chris through several years of his bodybuilding career and I recall reading an article where he was quoted as saying, "You never want to get to the point where you think you know more, or are better than the person who taught you." Chris eventually had his day. He went on to win more professional bodybuilding titles than anyone in the history of the sport.

The 1971 NABBA Professional Mr. Universe contest ended my almost twenty-year bodybuilding career. I had

contest. A young Belgian boy, about eleven years old, had been brought backstage, to see and possibly meet some of the contestants. The father nudged the boy, his autograph book in hand, toward Sergio. BIG MISTAKE! The moment the boy got into his space, Sergio shouted something like, "Get the hell out of here! I don't have time for autographs! See me after the show!" The outburst shocked the father and son to the point where you could actually see dismay on their faces.

Regaining his composure, the father began pushing the boy toward me. The boy walked over, his head down, autograph book at arm's length, afraid to make eye contact. Having seen the crestfallen look on the child's face, I signed my name and then picked him up and placed him on my shoulder as he flexed his skinny arm while his father snapped a photograph.

The next time I saw his father, he was looking at me while sitting at the judge's table with a smile on his face, nodding his head up and down, mouthing the word, "Yes--yes--yes."

The following day, Cecil Peck, the Master of Ceremonies, announced Bill Pearl as the overall winner of the 23rd annual NABBA Professional Mr. Universe contest. The audience roared its approval, but some of the major contestants apparently felt differently. Frank Zane,

Bill Pearl with a young Belgian fan, Chris Vandenbroele, backstage at the prejudging of the 1971 NABBA Professional Mr. Universe.

made the promise that if I got through it, I would be forever thankful.

My wife, Judy, and I returned to our normal lives in Pasadena, California, working in our gym twelve to fifteen hours a day. The only fanfare was a nice write-up in the Pasadena Star News and the members of the club surprised us with a party and a gift of a flintlock rifle, which I hung on our office wall. All requests for articles, exhibitions and seminars were turned down. My competitive bodybuilding career had gone full circle from being elated at winning the 1953 AAU Mr. America contest to wanting to forget the 1971 NABBA Mr. Universe contest. Competitive bodybuilding had changed into a sport that I no longer wanted to be a part of. With growing disappointment, I had watched the sport of fitness become a drug-based, dog-eat-dog business. I was one of the few competitors onstage that day that wasn't taking any form of anabolic steroids.

The following is an article written by George Coates for *Iron Man* magazine in early 1971.

Why Bill Pearl is Entering the NABBA Mr. Universe By George Coates

Bill Pearl is almost 41 years old. He has once again decided to enter NABBA's famed Mr. Universe Contest to be held as usual in London in September. I'm sure many people are wondering why. Why should this man who has been at the top longer than any other physique star lay his hard-earned reputation as the world's best-built man on the line against fellows half his age?

There are many reasons. Bill, like a lot of other people, loves the sport he has done so well at for over 20 years. He hates to see the game being abused in any shape or form. He is particularly appalled at the methods certain top physique men are resorting to in their quest for greater muscle size. Bill has a 14-year-old son and he swears if his boy has to take drugs and do some of the other crazy things these physique men are doing, he would sooner his boy never touched a barbell.

We all know that so many young men have radically changed the course of their lives, always for the worse, through the use (or should I say OVERUSE) of tissue-building drugs. Rumour has it that some men in the weight game have actually died as a result of taking these drugs. Bill wants to do all in his power to rid the weight game of DIANABOL and its counterparts. These drugs have their part in medicine, but they are NOT needed by ANYONE who desires to be healthy, fit and strong through the use of barbells!

Another reason that Bill has decided to enter this, his final contest, is due to the fact that for years he has silently endured ridicule and uncouth comments by a certain magazine with "the trainer of champions" at the helm. For years this magazine would provoke people like Bill, Reg Park and the one and only John Grimek by running "polls" to supposedly determine who was the world's greatest bodybuilder. In the final ratings, all three would appear way down their list. It got to be quite ridiculous! They would be rating men who would look like boys standing next to this trio of giants way up on their top ten, or top twenty, or whatever.

Last year things came to a head when an article was published attributed to Arnold Schwarzenegger, hurling rather unwarranted remarks at certain top liners, most of these being aimed at Bill Pearl in particular. I know Arnold Schwarzenegger. He would never write an article of that nature. He is a nice young man with a fantastic physique, currently associated with an organization that took similar advantages of Reg Park many years ago. In fact, Arnold and Earl Maynard (Mr. "U" of 1964) were visiting Leo Stern and me about six weeks ago, and believe me, big Arnold has nothing but the utmost respect and admiration for Bill Pearl. Being the gentleman he is however, Arnold would not comment.

Bill knows the only way he can compete fairly against anyone will be on neutral ground with fair and impartial judging. In other words, the NABBA Mr. Universe Contest!

Late last year, Bill and Leo Stern embarked on a one-year plan to prepare Bill and have him in the greatest shape of his life to compete in London. They had spared no efforts in this their final and most important undertaking. Every two weeks Bill and Leo get together and I feel deeply honoured to be allowed the privilege of attending most of these meetings, as the three of us will be associates in producing many magazine articles in the future.

To say Bill looks fantastic right now would be a gross understatement. As I write, the annual Mr. California Contest to be held in Los Angeles is only three days away. Bill is the guest poser in what may be his last public appearance in the United States. Most of the drug users will be in the audience and I will state here and now Bill will shock them right out of their seats.

Leo took some pictures of him last weekend and he is in unbelievable condition. You will be seeing some of these pictures soon. *After the Mr. Universe Contest is over Bill and Leo will be disclosing some of the methods Bill has used to attain this fantastic condition. One or two phases of Bill's preparation for the Mr. Universe contest are closely guarded secrets and will be told after the great event.*

Bill and Leo both hope all the top liners enter this year to decide once and for all the question, "Who is undeniably the greatest of the modern day bodybuilders?" I know one thing for sure and so does Bill, they don't play favourites in London. You have to be the best man there or you don't win. People like Oscar Heidenstam, Bert Loveday, Colin Sheard, Hal Wrigley and the rest of the judging panel are the most knowledgeable in the world.

I sincerely hope Bill Pearl can do it! I personally hope he can bump off the very best of the drug users and anyone else on the scene besides.

While the rest of the bodybuilding world awaits with bated breath what could prove to be the greatest ever NABBA Mr. Universe contest, Bill Pearl will be training with a vengeance and a quest. The quest being to put the game back on its feet where it belongs. To show everyone connected with the game that it's possible to attain the physique they desire without resorting to the dangerous practice of using drugs. In this writer's humble opinion, it's not only dangerous, it's absolute madness. Bill Pearl will be using the sane and sensible methods he has always believed in with one or two innovations, which will be made public at a later date. I hope all readers of this magazine will join me in wishing Bill Pearl success in his final venture as a physique contestant.

George Coates in the early 1960s. George and Bill have been friends since the start of Bill's bodybuilding career. He was a contributing author for a number of physique magazines.

Waverley
BELLE
CYCLES
The QUEEN
of LADIES'
CYCLES
SUPERB
CONSTRUCTION
Light weight, Artistic
Lines—just what ladies need.
Waverley
BICYCLE CO.
$90

Chapter II

SUPERMAN? NOT!

You Tell On Yourself

You tell on yourself by the friends you seek,
By the very manner in which you speak,
By the way you employ your leisure time,
By the use you make of dollar and dime.
You tell what you are by the things you wear,
And even by the way you wear your hair,
By the kind of things at which you laugh,
By the records you play on your phonograph.
You tell what you are by the way you walk,
By things of which you delight to talk,
By the manner in which you bury deceit,
By so simple a thing as how you eat.
By the books you choose from the well-filled shelf.
In these ways and more you tell on yourself.

Author Unknown

In late 1972, the idea struck me to take up competitive cycling. Like most transitions in life, my competitive cycling began as something else entirely. Judy and I bought bikes to take weekend rides and soon it became a group thing, with several members of the gym riding along. Then I was invited to join a group of competitive cyclists who raced a 30-mile circuit around the Rose Bowl on Tuesday afternoons. I upgraded to a $3,000.00 customized bicycle and changed my leg workout weekday mornings to include a 35-mile course around Pasadena, Altadena, South Pasadena and Sierra Madre. I left Sundays open for other races or 100-mile "century" rides. My enthusiasm for cycling went on for nearly four years.

Two of my cycling partners, Dr. Jeff Spencer and Chuck Pranke, were U.S. Olympic cyclists. Both were great teachers, but never in my wildest dreams did I come close to reaching their ability. One year I managed to place in the senior division of the California State Championships before my over-enthusiasm began causing problems. Coming home from a long Sunday ride, I discovered Judy wasn't waiting. "Where in the hell is she? It's our only day off and she's not here." This went

on for several months before coming to an impasse. After listening to my complaints, she calmly went to a drawer to take out a pen and pad. "Do both of us a favor," she said. "Write down the number of hours you work in the gym each week." I wrote down sixty hours. "How much time are you spending on the bike each week?" Another twenty-seven hours. "What about your weight training?"

A 19-pound bicycle supporting a 230-pound Bill Pearl.

Left: A Waverly Belle Cycle advertising poster from 1876, which is part of Bill's bicycle memorabilia.

I added an additional twelve hours. It came close to a hundred hours each week that I was either spending on myself or working in the gym. She calmly asked, "With the added time you spend for sleeping and eating, where do I fit in?"

To make matters worse, Judy was working longer hours at the gym, covering for me. I'd begun having health problems. Cysts had developed in my colon and had become abscessed. I refused to see a doctor, thinking the problem was hemorrhoids. Cutting back on cycling didn't help. Every time I rode, or lifted weights, my shorts filled with blood. Afraid to see a doctor, thinking "colon cancer," eventually it got to the point where I couldn't work more than a few hours each day. Then a rumor began that I did have cancer. We began getting phone calls from around the country asking if the gym was for sale. Most of the intended buyers were hoping to steal it.

If it could be ridden, then Bill was interested.

Something had to be done. Pain drove me to see a proctologist, chosen from the telephone yellow pages. Without any preliminaries, the doctor led me into a small room, had me lie on an examining table with my pants and underwear around my knees with my rear end hanging over the side. Applying a rubber glove, he smeared the middle finger with Vaseline. Without warning, he drove the finger up my ass to his elbow. My next memory was of lying on the floor, looking up, screaming, "You son-of-a-bitch! You just lost a customer!"

Harold Bailey, M.D., a true friend and longtime member of our Manchester Gym, came to my rescue. His more gentle examination discovered four large cysts that had gotten so badly abscessed he immediately arranged for surgery. While recovering, the realization hit that I was just as mortal as the next person, but far more self-centered. Once less time was spent at the gym, along with less time on my so-called hobbies, domestic problems were a thing of the past.

This page has been intentionally left blank.

L. Paul Coble ~ Colalie

Chapter III

MY FORMATIVE YEARS

From the poem "Roofs"
They say that life is a highway,
And its milestones are the years;
And now and then there's a tollgate,
Where you buy your way with your tears.

It's a rough road and a steep road,
And it stretches broad and far,
But at last it leads to a golden town
Where the golden houses are.

Joyce Kilmer

I was born on the Warm Springs Indian Reservation near Prineville, Oregon, October 31, 1930. My father, born, Harold Frank Pearl in 1903, my mother, born, Mildred Elizabeth Pasley in 1905, were primarily of American Indian descent. They were seventeen and fifteen years old, respectively, when they married. My sister, Fontelle, is four years older than my brother, Harold, who is three years older than me.

Dad was fair haired, fair skinned, never weighing more than 185 pounds at a height of six feet. He was nervous and always expected the worst, which caused him to suffer from a lifelong negative attitude. While growing up, the abuse and lack of love he experienced were the cause for much of his bitterness. His mother died when he was very young and his father had better things to do than to raise him. His grandmother took on the responsibility, until she died when he was 10-years old.

Dad was then shuttled back and forth between two uncles. Their only interest in him was as cheap labor. It was common for them to come home drunk and physically abuse him. He did chores before school, after school and had weekends to catch up. At fourteen, he rebelled; quit school, hired out as a field hand for room and board and very little pay. By the time I graduated from high school, he owned several restaurants, taverns, pool rooms, card rooms, pinball / jukebox / slot machine routes, clothing stores, a lumber mill and a producing gold mine near Grangeville, Idaho.

Because of his bitterness, little was known about his side of our family. As a teenager, I recall hearing him tell my mother that his father was still alive and residing in Seattle, Washington. Apparently, he had remarried and

Bill has never claimed to be camera shy.

Left: A young Bill Pearl with a gleam in his eyes toward his future.

Bill and his father, Harold, in the mid 1960s.

fathered siblings we hadn't met. My only association with his family came decades later while I was doing a guest appearance at a fitness store in Seattle. A sweet older lady introduced herself by saying, "I'm your father's younger sister." My response was, "You must be mistaken. My father doesn't have a sister." She then began reeling off my mother's maiden name, the names of Fontelle, Harold, along with other information that only a family member would know. She gave me a telephone number soliciting my promise to pass it on to dad. The two eventually made contact. The later years of his life were much happier because of their close association.

There is no doubt that my father's negativism influenced our relationship. I never felt confident about approaching him with questions or problems. Our first meaningful dialogue occurred in my early twenties while we were exchanging comments on an upcoming presidential election. For the first time, I realized that he was speaking to me as an equal. Prior to this, the one-sided conversations were usually something on the line of, "You goddamned kids drive me crazy!"

One of his major complaints was my obsession for weight training. He couldn't believe my time wouldn't be better spent doing something more productive. The more he complained, the more determined I became to prove him wrong. In his defense, some of his finer attributes were: being a self-starter, working for himself, not being afraid of challenges and being self-reliant--traits I'm glad to have inherited.

My relationship with my mother was the opposite. It was one of love. I always sought her advice when something important weighed on my mind. They spent their last years in Union Gap, Washington, two blocks from my sister and brother-in-law. Mom passed away at the age of seventy-five while sitting in her special chair,

saying she wanted to take a long nap. She deserved it; she had virtually worked herself to death. Dad's final years were spent making wooden animals out of scrap lumber. Each masterpiece was equipped with revolving legs or wings that spun when caught in a wind. He sold to all comers by displaying his wares on the front fence of their home. He died at the age of ninety-three, leaving two dogs and thirteen cats for my sister, Fontelle, and my brother-in-law, Phil, to care for.

My earliest memories were of chaos and confusion. It seemed my folks were always working. Around the age of three or four, I'd wake up most nights knowing my folks weren't home and cried. This would irritate Fontelle and Harold, which caused me to cry even harder. When my parents were home, they'd be so exhausted that all they wanted to do was sleep. Eventually, they got so tired, Dad sold the business to rest. During these breaks, our home life was as normal as could be expected. When it came time to go back to work, they were usually ready. The constant fighting and arguing amongst Fontelle, Harold and myself was enough to drive anyone back to work. Yet, all the blame can't fall on us. We were used to fending for ourselves and survived by any means possible.

Some of my fonder early memories came from my folk's sporadic domestic separations. Usually Mom would take us to Chelan, Washington, to stay with her mother, Cora, our very understanding grandmother. Grandma was extremely independent and a disciplinarian. She lived alone in the middle of nowhere, in a brown-shingled house that was surrounded by apple orchards. Life with her was definitely more structured than the way we lived in Yakima. Her right eye had been injured and removed

Bill's dad in his late 80s with his half-sister, Evelyn Gerdes.

Bill's mother, Mildred, in her later years.

when she was a teenager. To cover the injured area, she wore an eye patch. Being so young and not knowing what had happened, I would ask if her eye was getting better. She'd always smile and answer, "Yes."

Memories aren't nearly as pleasant when recalling another of their intermittent separations. I was preschool age, which makes circumstances more vague. What I remember is being outside in the dead of winter with my folks screaming at each other, as I was dragged between them. Dad must have won because the "three kids" were now staying with this cantankerous old bitch, Mrs. Bunton. We may have been there for a few months or a few weeks; it seemed like forever. We stayed in a small room that was separated from the main house. The only heat came from a wood stove. Fontelle and Harold would split wood before school; my job was to carry it in and to keep the fire burning. Mrs. Bunton would waltz in to toss a box of dry cereal on the table for breakfast and seldom be seen again, until she served bologna sandwiches and Kool-Aid for supper.

Every three or four days, Dad would drop by to give Fontelle and Harold school-lunch money. His route, servicing pinball machines throughout Washington State, was the reason he gave for not spending more time with us. Mrs. Bunton would appear the minute he drove away and the money would be gone.

The only visit Mother made was a few days after I burned my leg by falling against the stove during a night trip to use the bathroom. Mrs. Bunton was so busy counting her stolen change she hadn't attended to the burn, which had become infected. When Mom saw how badly I'd been injured, we were out of there.

For most of our maturing years, the task of motherhood fell on Fontelle's shoulders. The three of us were assigned chores, but Harold and I learned that what we didn't do, Fontelle would. When she tried to control us, our response was to give her the "bird" or swear at her. This would upset her even more. Having to share the same bedroom with us until she was in her early teens didn't help. Harold and I slept in the nude knowing it added to her misery. One of the few things in her favor was the standing rule that neither Harold nor I were allowed to hit her, especially in the chest, because she was "developing." Yet, there was no rule about her hitting us. When she did hit, it wasn't an open-handed slap, but a punch to knock our lights out. Our salvation was to outrun her; however, that seldom worked. She had learned to throw heavy objects with extreme accuracy.

Harold didn't fare any better making it to adulthood. In his early years, he was a true loner who spent most of his time staring out windows. He dropped out of school after the 8th grade, not because of the lack of intelligence, but because of boredom. He felt he could do better than sitting in a classroom waiting for something to happen. When he did get involved in a specific project, it was carried to the absolute end. An example would be that from the time he quit school until this day, he carries a

Bill's mom and dad in the kitchen of their restaurant in Missoula, Montana, in the late 1950s.

25

Harold, Fontelle and Bill, being nice enough to each other to have a picture taken.

like this sum up the differences between the two of us.

The only athletic endeavor we took part in together was learning to box. Ed Hale, our Native American landlord, started the Adam's Street Boxing Club in an abandoned storage area in our low-income neighborhood. Had there been State-aid or welfare, at least 65-75 % of the families living in our area would have qualified. The scar tissue around his eyes was proof that Mr. Hale had learned to box the hard way. He didn't charge to belong to the club. Every youngster who lived close by was welcome to participate in the boxing lessons, the roadwork, sit-ups, push-ups and tossing the medicine ball.

Some of the club's expenses were covered by "passing the hat" at the Friday-Night Fights, when the neighborhood came to watch the scheduled matches. Our opponents were kids we sparred with, or from the YMCA and the surrounding Indian reservations. Harold was the best boxer at the Adam's Street Boxing Club. He had uncanny body language, along with being left-handed.

Rather than improving our relationship, boxing made it worse. If we just looked at each other, it was time to fight. Any body contact caused fists to fly. The main reason I began weight training at such an early age (10-years old) was to get strong enough to defend myself against him. That was my short-term goal! My long-term goal was to get even stronger to kick his ass! Harold knew my intentions, so he began weight training to keep ahead

pocket dictionary. Any unfamiliar word (spelling or definition) is looked up and memorized.

The three of us worked in most of my folk's restaurants. We normally worked three or four nights a week and either a Saturday or Sunday. We didn't get paid; therefore, most summers were spent in hop fields or orchards. My parents didn't dictate how we spent, or saved, but would brag about how well I handled my money, compared to how Harold handled his. My money went to buy school clothes and to replenish a meager checking account, while Harold spent and saved more secretively. He stuck his money in a big woolen sock and hid it. He apparently grew tired of my folks bragging about how well "Billy" handled his money. One day he grabbed his woolen sock, threw it on the table saying, "Billy does things his way. I do things mine!" Incidents

Many years later, the three Pearls were able to smile about their childhood.

26

of me. Fortunately, by my thirteenth birthday we were close to the same stature. It then became the game of who got in the first blow, plus the most thereafter.

My fighting wasn't confined to the Adam's Street Boxing Club, or with Harold. It rolled over throughout my school years. One early altercation stands out more vividly than others. In the fourth grade, while playing soccer during recess, a boy wearing logger boots insisted on kicking me every chance he got. Mr. Elliott, the teacher refereeing the game, didn't interfere until I began punching my classmate. Perhaps because of my reputation, or the fact that I was getting the better of the fight, Mr. Elliott ran over to shove me around, as if the confrontation was entirely my fault. He threw up his guard, as if to take the boy's place. In retaliation, I threw a punch--a right that hit Mr. Elliott flush on the jaw. He went down like you wouldn't believe. Standing over him, I began thinking, "I'm in bad trouble! Knocking a teacher on his rear end isn't the smart thing to do." When Mr. Elliott gained his composure, he simply got up, looked at me, then walked away. That was it! No repercussions-- nothing--except that he stayed clear of me for the rest of my grammar school years. He eventually became one of my teachers in high school, but his lips remained sealed.

Chapter IV

ABSENCE OF MALICE

Three Gates

If you are tempted to reveal
A tale to you someone has told
About another, make it pass,
Before you speak, three gates of gold.
These narrow gates: First, "Is it true?"
Then, "Is it needful?" In your mind
Give truthful answer. And the next
Is last and narrowest, "Is it kind?"
And if to reach your lips at last
It passes through these gateways three,
Then you may tell the tale, nor fear
What the result of speech may be.

Author Unknown

Most summers of my early teens, Harold and I hired out to work in local orchards or hop fields. We tagged along with our neighbors, the Miller family, in their beat-up 1934 Chevrolet, four-door sedan. The automobile transportation ended when Hattie Miller, the mother, rolled the car when she fell asleep at the wheel. Fortunately, nobody was badly injured. Everyone's transportation was then limited to bicycles. It wasn't unusual to ride twenty miles to and from work. To avoid the heat of the day, Harold and I began at 3:00 a.m. and quit around noon. This meant getting up around 1:00 a.m. to be on time.

Returning home one afternoon, a passing car crashed into Harold. His left leg became tangled in the car's rear bumper, which somehow whipped him as high as a telephone pole before he hit the pavement. He spent several days in the hospital with a brain concussion and broken bones. The more lasting effects were that he seemed even more reclusive and withdrawn after the accident.

One evening, Mr. Miller got drunker than usual and raised more hell than normal, before neighbors phoned the police. That night ended with him shooting and killing the intervening police officer. Months later, he was convicted of first-degree murder. Years later, he had the

honor of being the last person the State of Washington executed by hanging. Hattie was left to raise her four children by whatever means were possible.

Before and after the tragic event, all of us Pearl kids spent more time at the Millers' home than we did at our own. Genevieve Miller, the oldest of the three daughters, was Fontelle's best friend. Don Miller was Harold's age and a friend to both of us. When we stayed overnight, which was often, it was common to wake up to a plate of pinto beans supplemented by day-old bread.

On Don's sixteenth birthday, he and Harold joined the United States Merchant Marines, where they spent two years in the South Pacific before they then enlisted in the U.S. Army for an additional three years. Don's goal was to save enough money to enable him to pay for a college education when he was discharged. He regularly sent money to Hattie to deposit in a savings account; instead, she used it to help support the family, or for Saturday night binges. He returned home to find his dreams of a higher education flushed down the drain.

Don and Harold had been discharged only a few months when the daily newspaper decided to do a follow-up on the family of the last person to be put to death by the State of Washington. All of the grief the Miller's had tried to put behind them was, again, to become front-page

Left: The early teens provided valuable lessons for Bill. Life was not a bowl of cherries.

Don Miller and Bill's brother Harold around 1943.

Pasadena, in 1969, it was the same. During all the years we worked together, it was a daily battle of who could get to whom first. Our hard-core fighting had ended, but by noon of each day we were either shaking our heads in disgust, or with laughter. A truce was accomplished around 1975 when Judy and I moved to southern Oregon, while Harold remained in the Los Angeles area.

Years would go by where the two of us would not hear from each other. In the year 2002, I phoned Harold saying, "I'm going to be in the Los Angeles area to receive the Spirit of Muscle Beach Award. Would it be okay if I stopped by to say hello?" (I would never dream of showing up unannounced.) "Hell yes," he said, "You can stay with us." I was so shocked by the invitation, I blurted out, "No! No! I can't stay with YOU." He asked, "Why can't you stay with US?" After a brief thought, I replied, "I don't know--I guess there's no reason why I can't stay with you." The next few days were some of the best we ever spent together. He graciously accompanied me to the Venice Beach awards ceremony. I was more than happy to share that small part of my life with Harold. His pounding on me throughout our childhood was the prime motivator to get me to where I am today.

news.

Before the story broke, the "old gang" decided to meet at Sam's house for a beer party. As the evening progressed, Don asked, "Hey Sam, you still got that pistol I loaned you before I went into the Army?" Sam replied, "Yeah, it's around here somewhere." Sam found the gun and handed it to Don saying, "Its still loaded so be careful." A few beers later, Don walked to the middle of the room, stuck the pistol to his head and blew his brains, along with portions of his skull, over all of us.

Harold was so upset over Don's death, he moved to southern California. He continued weight training regularly, getting in such great physical condition he could have won major physique contests, if it hadn't been something his little brother was planning to do. When I opened my first health club in Sacramento, California, in 1953, Harold became my first employee. In 1960, I purchased George Redpath's Gym in Los Angeles and Harold came along. When we opened our last club in

This page has been intentionally left blank.

Chapter V

WHAT AM I DOING HERE?

A Diamond in the Rough

A diamond in the rough is a diamond, sure enough,
And before it ever sparkled it was made diamond stuff.
But someone had to find it or it never would be found,
And someone had to grind it or it never would be ground.
But it's found, and when it's ground,
And when it's burnished bright,
That diamond's everlastingly giving out it's light.

O teachers of our young folk,
Don't say you've done enough;
It maybe that your rudest is
A diamond in the rough.

Author Unknown

Nobody took the time to tell me why I had to go to school. If someone had explained that it was a place to go to learn, it would have made sense. For me, it was a place to roost, until my folks came home from work.

Getting started was a series of difficulties. Most youngsters began school at the age of six, but because my birthday is in late October this meant waiting an extra year. For some reason that I've never understood, they placed me in kindergarten rather than the first grade. That alone was enough to make me hate school. Kindergarten sucked; all we did was play with toys and the one thing I hated most was, "You have to share." I'd fallen in love with a giant top that had a handle you pushed down to make it spin and whistle. The faster you pushed, the faster and louder it spun and whistled. I was always first at the toy box to grab the top, and then take my place on the floor next to the door of the coatroom to begin pumping away. The teacher would eventually have enough and retrieve it, either to give it to someone else, or to place it back in the box. That would be it for school that day. At the first chance for escape, I was gone. Thinking there was nothing better to do, I'd wander the neighborhood. I had decided that looking in backyards, garages and old barns was far more interesting than sitting in a classroom waiting for a bell to ring.

I was expelled from school in the second grade. Going home for lunch on this occasion, the only things in the refrigerator that looked appealing were two 8-ounce bottles of Olympia beer. I drank the beer and headed back to school. I had been strategically seated in the front of the class where the teacher could keep an eye on me. That day she did a better than average job. I sat with my chin in my hand, my elbow on the desk, stupidly smiling at her. When my elbow slipped, she got the idea that something was amiss. For this unbelievable misbehavior, I was suspended from school for the rest of the week. On my first day back in class, they put me in with a group of "special" students who got a half pint of milk and a graham cracker during morning recess. Still, I wasn't happy; my graham cracker usually came broken in half and the halves didn't match.

Conditions didn't improve in the third grade. Walking away at recess or lunchtime so often led to the school's presenting an ultimatum: either I had to take the grade over, or attend summer school. Mom opted for summer school. At the rate things were going, she was afraid I'd be older than the teacher by the time I graduated from high school.

Two things kept me somewhat interested in school: learning to play the saxophone in the third grade and the game of marbles. Playing marbles with hard-core classmates was as challenging as learning to play the instrument. We played the game from early spring until the first snow. We played on the way to school, during recess, lunch hour and on our way home. It was normal to have the knuckles on our shooting hands so heavily callused the dirt wouldn't wash off. If there weren't holes in the knees of our trousers, we weren't considered serious contenders.

On the way to school, we played the game called tag. Your opponent would stop to shoot his marble a few feet ahead. It was your job to shoot and hit his marble with yours. If you succeeded, his marble belonged to you. If you missed, it was his turn to try to do the same.

If you were smart, you never used your good shooter when playing tag. The game was too risky. You only used marbles you could afford to lose. A good shooter was like a prized pool cue; it stayed in a special place only to be used on special occasions. My good shooter was a sight to behold. It was made from pure agate; a beautiful golden brown with several rings around it plus a gorgeous built-in moon. It cost fifty cents, which at that time was a fortune.

The most popular game of marbles was called Bull Ring. Bull Ring was a good way to win, or lose, a handful of marbles in a hurry. To play the game, you drew a circle on the ground about six feet in diameter. Each player then anted up the same number of marbles to toss into the middle of the circle. Next, a lag line was drawn. Each player stepped backward a certain distance before aiming his marble at the line. The player's shooter that got the closest was the first to start the game.

The game began with the first person shooting from anywhere along the outside line of the circle. If his shooter hit one of the anted marbles and knocked it out of the circle, while his shooter stayed in the circle, the marble knocked out belonged to him. He continued shooting until he failed to knock a marble out of the circle or until his shooter went out the circle. However, if his shooter didn't go out of the circle on his last attempt, the next player had the option of trying to hit his shooter to knock it out of the circle. If he succeeded, and his shooter stayed in the circle, it was sudden death; you were out of the game. Your anted marbles were history.

The big day had arrived. The playground was filled with classmates. I was competing for the over-all winner in the marble playoff tournament for my grammar school. A 6-foot circle, plus the lag line, had been drawn in white chalk. My opponent had tossed a dozen marbles into the ring to equal mine. The privilege of shooting first belonged to me. I was hot! My beautiful agate knocked two anted marbles out of the white chalked circle. This continued until only six marbles were left. Poor judgment caused me to miss my next shot. My agate stopped six inches inside the curved chalked line. (A very dangerous place for my agate to be.) My opponent took out a steel ball bearing about the size of a quarter. (We called them steelies.) He went down on his knees, wrapped a part of his first finger around the front of the steelie, and then cocked his thumb behind the rear. He placed his callused knuckles on the white chalk line before letting his steelie fly. It hit my agate with such force that my marble flew out of the circle with several feet to spare. That was it! The game was over. He had won. I had lost. My first reaction was to kill! Not because of bad sportsmanship but because his steelie had knocked a chip out of my beautiful agate. Regardless of how the game ended, the chip was never going to go away. If you were to visit my office today, you will not see a series of physique trophies on display, but you will see a giant glass jar filled with more than two thousand marbles sitting on a shelf with my faithful agate resting on top, nicely wrapped in cotton, waiting for a miraculous recovery.

This page has been intentionally left blank.

Chapter VI

THE BUDDING ENTREPRENEUR

My Grandad
My grandad, viewing earth's worn cogs,
Said things are going to the dogs.
His grandad in his house of logs,
Said things are going to the dogs,
His grandad in the Flemish bogs,
Said things are going to the dogs,
There's one thing I have to state:
The dogs have had a good long wait!

Author Unknown

As a youngster I never had enough money to do things correctly. I loved anything that was mechanical, especially if it could be driven or ridden. Our house on Willow Street in Yakima, Washington, looked like a junk yard. Beat-up cars, motorcycles and bicycles encircled the property. Most of the cars on display were Model T Fords waiting for repair. Dad detested having trash everywhere. He nearly exploded when I drove home a ton-and-a-half flatbed truck that I parked on the front lawn. He sputtered, "I wish you'd get rid of those goddamned wrecks, along with the rest of the junk you got scattered all over the place! Why do you keep buying that crap?" I replied, "Dad! That's a good truck! You can haul all kinds of stuff to the dump!" His reply, "If I can't drive one of those things, how in the hell am I going to haul anything?" He had never learned to drive a vehicle with a transmission operated by three pedals.

I began dragging vehicles home in my pre-teens. My current collection has leveled off at thirty-two restored antique or classic automobiles, a few ancient motorcycles, Ingo cycles, motor scooters and several dozens of old ballooned-tired bicycles. Some of the older automobiles that are now in my compilation include an 1899 Marlboro Steam car, a 1907 Model N Ford, a 1908 Buick, a 1909 Ford and a 1910 Stanley Steamer.

My first automotive purchase was a 1924 Model T Ford touring car that had no seats, top or upholstery. I paid $2.00 for the car when I was eleven years old. It had been stored in a barn and used as a roost for chickens. The

birds had filled the body with their droppings. It took me days to dig out their remains and months to get the car to run. I "overhauled" the engine, found seats at a wrecking yard, rewired the lights, hooked a cow bell to the front axle, a red kerosene railroad lantern to the rear axle, and then drove it without a driver's license until I was sixteen years old.

My next major transportation investment occurred in 1943. The owner of Hank's Bicycle Emporium had a 1936 Austin Bantam automobile stored in the back room of his shop. The tiny car was so cute; I'd go to the shop just to look at it. On one visit, the shop repairman came to work with a 1937 Cushman motor scooter loaded in the back of his pickup truck. The scooter had been neglected for years. He mentioned it was for sale. I mentioned, "I've got two nice Schwinn bicycles I'll trade." He agreed. I rushed

A 1924 Model T Ford that Bill bought for $2.00 when he was eleven years old. He drove the car regularly without a drivers license until he was sixteen, and then failed the drivers test.

Left: Bill on one of his early modes of transportation, a 1937 Cushman motor scooter.

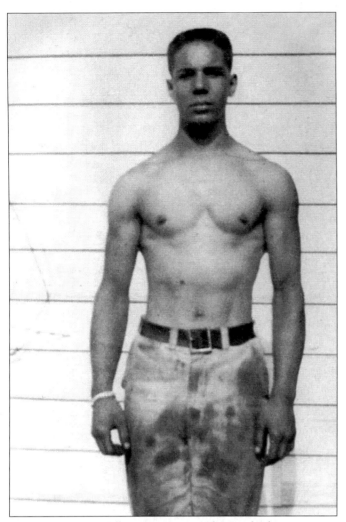

The grease stains on Bill's trousers are an indication that his transportation had oil leaks. Bill commented, "Those were my school pants."

home to tell Dad the good news. His response was, "NO! You'll never get the damned thing to run. It'll just sit here with the rest of that junk." His words fell on deaf ears.

I cleaned carbon off of the scooter's cylinder head, replaced the spark plug and wire, flushed out the gas tank, blew out the lines, cleaned the carburetor, changed the oil, replaced the brake and gas cables. Then I repainted it with green and yellow John Deere paint that was sprayed on by using a fly-spray applicator.

My biggest problem was tires. I not only didn't have money to buy tires, but finding them was nearly impossible. Because of World War II, everything was rationed: food, gasoline, leather, rubber goods, you name it. My brother-in-law came to the rescue. Through some military contact, he was able to get the correct tires and tubes. I skipped school the day they arrived to mount them.

For the next several years I rode the scooter everywhere without major mechanical problem. Eventually, I sold it back to the repairman for $250.00. Dad

was so impressed, he promised to never question my business judgment again.

The most fascinating automobile I encountered by my continual snooping as a youngster remains a sad memory. Weekend mornings, I'd either drive the Model T, or ride the scooter through alleys looking for anything old that was hidden in backyards, garages or barns. By chance, I peeked through a knothole of a crumbling barn to find an automobile so ancient, it used a tiller for steering. I immediately rushed to the front door of the house. An older man greeted me with a giant frown as if to say, "What in the hell do you want?" With every other breath calling him, 'SIR,' I told him of my love for antique automobiles, then finished by asking, "Is it possible to see the car that is stored in your barn?" My charm worked. The carriage turned out to be the first automobile registered in the State of Washington, a 1903 Curved Dash Oldsmobile. It had spent its last 40 years, in the darkness of the barn resting on blocks.

For the next two years, I did everything imaginable to get Mr. Smothers to part with the car. I worked on his house, mowed his lawn, pulled weeds, took him shopping, and drove him to doctor's appointments, all the time doing it with an ulterior motive...I wanted that car. I eventually resigned myself to the fact that I was never going to be able to buy the car. My next plan of attack was to continue to be so overly nice that Mr. Smothers would take pity and GIVE me the car.

On a bright Saturday morning I stopped, once again, to take Mr. Smothers shopping. A truck with out-of-state license plates was backed up to the barn. The driver was winching the Curved Dash Oldsmobile onto a trailer. I watched the loading process until the back of the old Oldsmobile disappeared down the alley. My desire to please Mr. Smothers disappeared as quickly. I had been taught a good lesson at an early age; wanting is one thing-

Bill loved anything that could be driven or ridden.

-getting is another.

Out of all the cars I've restored as an adult, my favorite is our 1909 one-cylinder Brush. The body, axles, frame, wheels and running boards were made of wood and only good for patterns. The rear wheels were chain driven, the engine and transmission apart in boxes. I paid a ridiculous price of $5,000.00 for the car. What I bought were parts.

The only convenient place on our property to restore the Brush was in the recreation room of our home. The rest of my collection filled the available covered areas on the property. When the restoration was completed, the Brush had to be dismantled to get it through the front door.

"Before and After" photographs of a 1909 one-cylinder Brush that Bill restored in the recreation room of their home.

The oldest car in Pearl's current auto collection: An 1899 Marlboro Steam Car.

A 1907 Model N Ford with right-hand drive.

Pearl's 1910 Model 10 Stanley Steamer.

Bill's 1909 Model T Ford is a rare car with a very low engine number.

Bill has owned this 1915 Model T Ford for over forty years. Bill and Judy have traveled thousands of enjoyable miles in this vehicle.

Restoring the 1909 one-cylinder Brush was a four-year project. Bill commented, "I can run almost as fast as it can go."

This page has been intentionally left blank.

Chapter VII

PERSPECTIVE

From the poem "The Power of Littles"
Great events, we often find,
On little things depend,
And very small beginnings
Have oft a mighty end....

Author Unknown

A major factor that enticed me into weight training, at the early age of ten, was hearing people comment on the size of my feet and hands. That didn't bother me as much as the remarks that came because of my giant head. The result of weighing 12 3/4 pounds at birth has had its lasting affect. I now weigh 235 pounds, wear size 12 EE shoes, my pinkie ring fits most people's thumbs and the only haberdashery that stocks hats large enough to fit my head is "Meyer the Hatter" located in New Orleans, Louisiana. Here's one example of how the size of my head has contributed to my ambition to build my body to match it. Fontelle found a hat left hanging on a coat hook near a back booth of the restaurant we owned, at closing time. Pop said it had to be new. For someone to have left the hat meant the owner wasn't accustomed to wearing it.

The hat was a gorgeous velvet gray fedora with a beautiful black satin band. The brim hung downward to duplicate the hat worn by Humphrey Bogart in the movie The Maltese Falcon. Stenciled on the inside sweatband were the numbers 7-7/8. The average hat size for men is between 6-1/4 and 7-1/8, which indicated that this hat had been designed to fit a huge head. My dad automatically tried it on. It was way too big. Harold was next; it covered his ears. Dad plopped it on my ten-year-old head to find it fit perfectly. He placed it back on the hook awaiting the owner's return.

Weeks later, I became the proud owner. For the next few winters while other kids wore stocking caps and fur lined earmuffs, I was stuck wearing my Humphrey Bogart look-alike. Considering I was extremely self-conscious about the size of my head, wearing the adult man's hat brought even more attention to the thing I was most sensitive about.

The "hat part" of my life ended on the evening our family went to dinner at the Golden Wheel restaurant in downtown Yakima. Dad drove his 1928 Pontiac coupe. The car had been converted into a makeshift pickup with room in front for three. We boys rode in the back with mother insisting, "Billy has to wear his hat to keep his head warm." We were ushered to a back booth equipped with a coat hook similar to the one in our restaurant. When the time came to leave, I was sure to be the last. With clear conscience, I left my Bogey Special hanging on the hook, just the way it had been left in our restaurant years before. My fervent prayer was that it would bring the next owner twice the pleasure it had bestowed upon me.

I recently told this story to a large group of firefighters attending the Phoenix, Arizona Fire Department Health and Fitness Training Seminar. Afterward, one of the attendees asked, "How long have you been training?" I replied, "This past August began my 62nd year. My hat size is still 7-7/8. The hang-ups I had, as a kid, are still with me today."

Left: The result of weighing 12 3/4 pounds at birth has had a lasting effect on Bill.

Chapter VIII

VICES

'The Circus'

Hey, there! Loop-la! the circus is in town!
Have you seen the elephant? Have you seen the clown?
Have you seen the dappled horse gallop round the ring?
Have you seen the acrobats on the dizzy swing?

Hoop-la Hoop-la! the circus is in town!

Hey, there! Hoop-la! Here's the circus troupe!
Here's the educated dog jumping through the hoop!
See the lady Blondin with the parasol and fan,
The lad upon the ladder and the india-rubber man.
See the joyful juggler and the boy who loops the loop.
Hey! Hey! Hey! Hey! Here's the circus troupe!

C. J. Dennis

For a few summers of my preteens, five or six of us from the neighborhood spent our days like primates, running nude, swimming, hanging from trees, taking mud baths and existing off of wild berries on a remote part of the Yakima River. During that time, it seemed fashionable for everyone to smoke. My folks were hooked on Pall Malls. I chose a broader selection by picking up butts off the street, not caring about brands. I smoked regularly for about three years before coming to my senses one extremely cold day, while hitchhiking with my brother-in-law from Yakima to Pasco, Washington. We became stranded in the middle of nowhere. I began complaining about the cold. He remarked, "Have a cigarette. It'll warm you up." Puffing away, I began thinking, "How stupid can I be? Puffing on a cigarette, thinking it is going to make things better, is ridiculous." I tossed it into the dirt to end my smoking career. Much less time was needed to cure me of chewing tobacco. I snitched a can of Skoal from our corner grocery store and broke the seal to the smell of sweet tobacco aroma. I filled my mouth and began to chew and swallow. In minutes, I was bent over heaving my guts out.

My life continued without much change. Harold kept pounding on me, my folks were gone most of the time and

Fontelle couldn't stand either of her brothers. My final decision to physically improve myself came by accidentally observing a circus strongman, just prior to the opening of the 1940 Washington State Fair. Living across the street from the Fairgrounds, I glanced out our front window and was shocked to see a giant African elephant standing next to the curb not twenty feet from our door. The handler was nowhere to be seen. There was no waiting to get a closer look. In a flash, I was out the door looking up at the biggest, most magnificent creature I had ever imagined. As I continued to study the animal, to my amazement, he slowly bowed his head to the left, and then with his trunk, gently tossed the handler high enough to allow him to land standing erectly on the elephant's back.

The handler immediately was transformed into a full-fledged circus strongman. Dressed in leopard-skin tights, roman-sandal shoes and a red form-fitting T-shirt, he peered down at me like a genie from a bottle. Once he recognized that he had my full attention, he graciously bowed before going into a handstand on the elephant's back. For the next several minutes the master performer completed one acrobatic feat after another. Then, without warning, he stopped, sat on the elephant's shoulders, and

Left: Twelve-year old Bill and his fifteen-year-old brother, Harold.

A circus strongman made such an impression on the young Bill Pearl, it became the incentive for him to begin physically improving himself.

gave a slight nudge with his knees, which caused the elephant to walk toward the entranceway to the fairgrounds. As they entered, the lumbering stride slowed as the strongman looked back and began waving his arm back-and-forth, as if motioning me to follow. I nearly died. "This guy wants me to follow! Maybe he'll teach me to become just like him. If he can do those amazing feats and is strong enough to control objects that seem bigger than life, then, sure as heck, he can teach me how to control my brother and find solutions for the rest of my problems." My folks felt differently. Our short conversation ended with, "NO!" But the decision was made. I wanted to grow up to be just like the strongman.

At the age of 72, Bill still had not forgotten the circus strongman from his childhood that made such an impact on his life.

This page has been intentionally left blank.

Chapter IX

SEEDS OF CHANGE

Life's Book
No matter what else you are doing,
From cradle days through to the end,
You are writing your life's secret story,
Each night sees another page penned.
Each month ends a thirty-page chapter;
Each year, the end of a part;
And never an act is misstated,
Nor even a wish of the heart,
Each morn when you wake, the book opens,
Revealing a page clean and white;
What thoughts and what words and what doings
Will cover its surface by night!
God leaves that to you...you the writer...
And never one word will grow dim
Until someday you write the word "finish"
And give back your life's book to Him.

Author Unknown

On Sunday morning, December 7, 1941, my small world began to make a significant change--not for the better. With our floor model Philco radio blaring away, the music stopped for a special report on the bombing of Pearl Harbor. America was at war with Japan. Until then, my friend Toshi Takamura and I were sure of meeting every morning, five days a week, to walk to and from school. We met at a small convenience store that sold cigarettes, candy, gum, soft drinks and comic books. We also ate lunch together in the school cafeteria. He was an "outsider" and my natural instinct was to protect him. He paid me back by sitting next to me in class to help me with my schoolwork. After school, if either of us had money, we'd share a candy bar or a soft drink.

The morning after the bombing, we met as usual, making sure that nothing was said about being at war. However, as we walked to school, someone driving by hollered, "You Lousy Jap!" Another, "Jap Lover!" At school, the teacher didn't call on Toshi to answer questions and the harassment he went through at recess made me even more determined to stick by him.

We continued meeting until the Christmas holidays. The first few mornings of the New Year, I was late for school waiting for him. I later found out Toshi, the one friend I could count on, had vanished from my life. His family had been shipped to an internment camp in central Oregon for the duration of the war.

Before long, due to rationing, the convenience store, where we had shared the after-school treats, also vanished. The war had begun taking its toll on my little world, causing me to become even more confused and resentful.

A year into the war, Dad closed the restaurant in Yakima. The difficulties caused by food shortages finally had taken their toll. We moved into a Victorian home on 13th and K Streets in Tacoma, Washington. Dad went to work for the Seattle/Tacoma Shipyards, building Kaiser Liberty Ships. The rest of us worked at becoming accepted in our new surroundings.

The neighborhood was predominantly Greek. Last names like Nitas, Doxikas and Topopolomus were as common as the name, Smith, in the rest of the United

Left: A poster made popular during World War I and still used in World War II.

States. None of the kids wanted anything to do with Harold or me. We were the neighbors with the funny last name who couldn't speak their language.

The isolation continued for nearly the entire school year before acceptance took place. A beautiful two-story Catholic church covered half of the block across the street from our school. One morning recess, Harold decided to climb onto the roof of the church to smoke a cigarette. Thirty minutes later, all of the school windows facing the church filled with eyes, watching the roof of the church go up in flames. Adding to the excitement, the outer wooden shingled walls soon joined the conflagration. As the fire grew, additional fire trucks arrived; next came newspaper reporters, taking pictures and asking questions. By the time the fire was extinguished, the only portion of the church left standing was its cement foundation.

Students were called to the principal's office. Someone had seen a boy climbing off the roof of the church on the day of the fire. They got around to questioning Harold. He admitted climbing on the roof, lighting a cigarette, flipping a match. "But," he asked, "What does that have to do with the church being set on fire?"

Harold became instantly famous. His unidentified name and admission to smoking on the roof of the church made headline news. Now all the kids in school and the neighborhood wanted to be like him even though we remained the brothers with the funny last name. By the time we departed Tacoma, both Harold's and my ability to speak the Greek language had improved immensely. There wasn't a Greek swear word that we couldn't enunciate as well as any Greek kid in the neighborhood.

Our family moved back to Yakima and, once again, we were in the restaurant business. Dad bought a cafe in the seedy part of downtown and a house on Willow and 7th Avenue. We lived there until I graduated from high school. The one-story full basement, rectangular box, was situated on a double sized lot. The basement was used to launch my bodybuilding career. I had finally figured out what was necessary to achieve my long-term goal. I had to begin lifting weights.

I began by reading books about old-time strongmen, how they trained and then attempted to emulate what they'd done. The transition from lifting anything that wasn't fastened down occurred when the $22.95 York Big Ten Special weight set I had ordered in late 1941 was

Bill's first set of weights was the York Big Ten Special. He ordered the set in late 1941.

Young school chums: Ed Parrish, Bill Pearl and Al Simmons.

We began working out in the basement three days a week. Our exercise bench was two heavy apple crates with a 2 x 12 inch board lying across them. Other than the training courses that came with the set, everything was trial and error. Fortunately, from the beginning, records were kept of every workout. I recorded our body weight, what exercises we did, how much weight was used and the number of sets and reps we performed. Every few months we'd analyze what seemed to be working, then adjust our training accordingly. I continued keeping accurate records for the next fifty years. Even with limited equipment, we made noticeable progress. By the ninth grade I was doing repetition one-arm snatches with a 100-pound barbell. As my size and strength increased, my mental attitude improved accordingly.

Al remained my hit-and-miss training partner all through junior and senior high school. During our last two years of school, we began training with two older, more advanced bodybuilders at the Yakima YMCA.

delivered in 1945. The York Big Ten Special consisted of eighty pounds of assorted weight plates, a five-foot bar, two dumbbell handles, collars, two kettle bell handles, a pair of iron boots and a wrist-roller.

By now, Al Simmons and I were seldom out of each other's sight. We were thirteen years old when we met and remained dear friends until his death in 1996. As a youngster, Al took me under his wing. I trusted nobody. His take on life was the opposite. He found good in everything. Al had the habit of kissing his parents hello and good-bye, while hugging everyone in between. Watching how he related taught me that if you are nice to people, they are usually nice in return; if you treat people with respect, they will usually treat you accordingly, and if you are going to discriminate, do it on an individual basis.

When notice came that the weight set was waiting at the freight docks, I didn't have $5.00 to pay the freight bill. A pact was made. If Al would help with the freight bill, we would become training partners, but, if he stopped training, he didn't get any part of The York Big Ten Special.

Bill and Al, fifty years later.

Chapter X

BUILDING BLOCKS OF CHARACTER

Looking Forward
I dream of a glorious future,
Of a bright and better day
When every living creature
God's mandates will obey;

When every man will find a friend
In every other man,
And each will seek the good of all
According to God's plan;

When enmity shall disappear,
And wars be waged no more,
But peace and love and beauty
Abound from shore to shore;

Ruth May Fox

The more involved I became in school, the more tolerable it became. Eventually my grades began to climb. I made the honor roll in high school, but if it hadn't been for music and sports, it's doubtful I would have stayed to graduate. Playing the saxophone, from the 3rd grade on, was one of the most significant events that could have happened. It gave me an interest. I wasn't a natural musician, but tenacity and constant practice paid dividends. I took part in band and orchestra all through school and my four-year Naval enlistment.

Jimmy Robinson was a natural. Everyone in his family was musically gifted. His older sister performed regularly in New York City Broadway Musicals. The younger brother was as talented as she. His parents operated a small, poorly stocked grocery store in the black area of Yakima. Mr. Robinson also acted as the lay minister for a one-room Protestant Church in that neighborhood. On Wednesday nights and Sunday mornings, the building would be rocking. Mr. Robinson would lead the small choir before preaching a rousing

sermon. Jimmy's mother played the piano and sang along, as the children accompanied them on different instruments. When asked, I'd bring my saxophone to take part in the festivities. I was usually the only non-black in the congregation.

Jimmy and I organized a dance band with three others from our junior-high school orchestra. We played together through our remaining school years. In the summers of our junior and senior years, Jimmy and I spent most Friday nights with an older Mexican musician playing for itinerant farm workers at Granges throughout the Yakima valley. One evening, before a Grange dance, we stopped at a little outdoor food stand to order a hamburger and a soft drink. My food quickly arrived. Waiting a few minutes, I remarked, "Excuse me, I believe you've made a mistake. We both ordered a hamburger and Coke." Pointing a finger at both of us, the waitress sarcastically replied, "We'll serve you, but we won't serve him!" Not believing what she had said, I asked her to repeat it. She barked, "We'll serve you, but we won't serve

Left: Bill with Richard Schiffner and Jimmy Robinson, singing their hearts out during a high school function.

55

him!" Jimmy stayed calm, as rage overcame me. Her words hit like she had spit in my face. The end results were the hamburger and Coke sailing across the counter, with me screaming what could be done with the bill.

The tables turned early one morning after we had played another outlying Grange. It was past 2:00 a.m. and all restaurants in Yakima were closed except for one in the black area of town. As we walked in and sat at the counter, all eyes zeroed in on me. Even though I counted on Jimmy to take care of me under such circumstances, it became less reassuring when this rugged-looking black man seated across the counter REALLY began staring. You could see his brain working as he reached his hand inside his upper-jacket pocket to pull out an object, just far enough to show what looked like the handle of a pistol, then shake his head as if deciding what to do, before sliding the object back into the pocket. This happened enough to make me more than nervous. I whispered in Jimmy's ear, "Watch that guy over there. He's got a gun in his jacket pocket. He's gonna' shoot me! Let's get the hell out of here!" Jimmy shook his head and replied, "No he doesn't have a gun. Just settle down. You're gonna' be okay." The tension continued to build as we ate our bowls of chili, but immediately eased as we got up to leave. My suspected assassin decided that it was now safe to pull out his flask to pour a shot of liquor into his coffee. My relief was so great I felt like going over to shake his hand, asking if he would share.

Bill continued his musical career during his four-year Naval enlistment. He can be seen in the first row, far right, playing a bass saxophone for the USS Nereus dance band.

This page has been intentionally left blank.

Chapter XI

EARLY ATHLETIC CAREER

Who Touches A Boy By The Master's Plan

Who touches a boy by the Master's plan
Is shaping the course of a future man,
Is dealing with one who is living seed
And may be a man whom the world will need.

Author Unknown

There wasn't a problem for me to win wrestling tournaments for the Yakima YMCA or lettering in most sports through school. Weight training made me stronger and more confident. Football wasn't my passion, but was a sure way of getting a higher education. Upon graduating from high school, several football scholarships became available. Offers came from the University of Washington and Washington State University, along with several smaller schools in our local area.

By now, wrestling had become more important than football, and almost as important as weight training. Al and I began wrestling while in junior high school. Norm Kelly, one of the advanced bodybuilders that we trained with at the YMCA, had taken us under his wing to teach us basic wrestling moves. In high school, we talked Norm Burke, a substitute teacher and former National Collegiate Wrestling Champion, into training with us at the Y. He was an even better coach than Norm Kelly. If there were problems taking us off our feet, he'd kick the outside of our knees until our legs gave way, or slap the sides of our heads until we were more than happy to give him the take down.

Mr. Burke's attitude was similar toward teaching school. Charles Lane, a student known for making teachers' lives miserable, was insistent on raising hell during a study hall session. Mr. Burke, acting as the study hall teacher, told him to stop. Chuck retaliated with a smart remark, which caused Mr. Burke to stand and motion him to step into the hall. Moments later, a loud crash was heard against the lockers and then a thump of something hitting the floor. Mr. Burke re-entered the room while adjusting his tie shouting, "Listen up! This job doesn't mean that much to me. I'm not going to put up

with any crap." I proudly listened to his remarks before saying to the kid sitting next to me, "Ain't he great? I work out with him three times a week!"

This week's athlete, a hero of the Marquette victory and a full-back on the YHS football team, is Bill Pearl 11L. Bill played one year as a tackle with the "B" squad before switching to the backfield and playing with

Bill lettered in track and field and football during his three years of high school.

Left: Throughout school, Al Simmons was Bill's weight training and wrestling partner. Al Simmons, Judy and Bill fifty-years later.

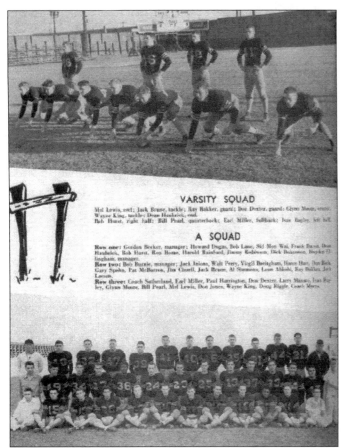

VARSITY SQUAD

Mel Lewis, end; Jack Bruse, tackle; Ray Bakker, guard; Don Dexter, guard; Glynn Moore, center; Wayne King, tackle; Dean Hauhrich, end.
Bob Howat, right half; Bill Pearl, quarterback; Earl Miller, fullback; Ivan Bagley, left half.

A SQUAD

Row one: Gordon Becker, manager; Howard Dugan, Bob Lane, Sid Mon Wai, Frank Dunn, Don Hauhrich, Bob Horst, Ron Home, Harold Rainford, Jimmy Robinson, Dick Boinsteon, Hayden Fillingham, manager.
Row two: Bob Burnie, manager; Jack Inions, Walt Perry, Virgil Breitghum, Haree Hart, Don Belt, Gary Spohn, Pat McBarron, Jim Cissell, Jack Bruse, Al Simmons, Leon Ahlsohl, Ray Bakker, Jack Larson.
Row three: Coach Sutherland, Earl Miller, Paul Harrington, Don Dexter, Larry Manaw, Ivan Bagley, Glynn Moore, Bill Pearl, Mel Lewis, Don Jones, Wayne King, Doug Riggle, Coach Moen.

Track Squad

first row: Claud Henle, Wendell Webb, Glenn Kampp, Jack Bloxom, Marsden Hunter, Don Beuter, Don Prowincha, Wayne Spurs, Dick Terrill; **second row:** Jack Eddy, Lee Englead, Bill Pearl, Ivan Bagley, Walt Searle, Chuck Baker, Delbert Keller, Sid Foley, Bob Schultz, Cecil Carrey, Cleo Stapleton; **third row:** Al Simmons, Ed Parrish, Bob Cheshire, Will Hughes, Stan Neper, Bill Mays, Bob Shannon, Gerald Hodge, Joe Pratt, Jack Bruse; **fourth row:** Stan Schoonover, Charley Waggoner, Glyn Moore, Ralph Long, Dean Hauhrich, Guy Shinn, James Jefferson, Kenneth Keller, Del Reynolds, Dick Thomas.

Foster Medley Relay

Walt Searle, Bill Pearl, Bob Foley, Delbert Keller.

880 Relay

Bill Pearl, Ralph Long, Bill Charbonneau, Chuck Baker.

In the "Varsity Squad" photograph Bill is standing, second from the left. Bill is in the back row, eighth from the left, in the "A Squad" photograph.

Bill can be found in the second row from the bottom, third from the left in the "Track Squad" photograph. Bill is standing second from the left in the "Foster Medley Relay" photograph and first from the left in the "880 Relay" photograph.

Bill and Al Simmons shaking hands. Wrestling had become almost as important as weight training.

Bill wearing his father's only dress suit, in 1946.

Bill's main mode of transportation during junior and senior high school.

STRENGTH & *Health*

Leo Stern

January
1950
25¢
30¢ IN CANADA

Chapter XII

A STEP TOWARD MANHOOD

The Few

The easy roads are crowded
And the level roads are jammed;
The pleasant little rivers
With the drifting folks are crammed,
But off yonder where it's rocky,
Where you get a better view,
You will find the ranks are thinning
And travelers are few.

Where the going's smooth and pleasant
You will always find the throng,
For many, more's the pity,
Seem to like to drift along.

But the steeps that call for courage,
And the task that's hard to do,
In the end result in glory
For the never wavering few.

Edgar A. Guest

In our sophomore year of high school, Al Simmons got the idea that we should join the United States Marine Corps Reserves. For the next three years, the government paid us a small amount each month for meeting Tuesday nights to watch old war movies--no training--just movies. Not long after graduation, the Korean War began. Our reserve unit was on the active list to be called overseas. Al and I quickly decided that going to Korea, as Marines, especially after watching three years of people being burned to death by flame throwers, wasn't the smartest move. During a lunch break from our summer job of teaching swimming at the local public pool, we visited the United States Naval Recruiting Office. Returning to the pool, Al jokingly mentioned that we had joined the Navy. To save face, we enlisted the following day. Dad's first comment was, "Do you realize how long two years can be?" I countered, "Pop, we didn't enlist for two years, we enlisted for four." Shaking his head in disgust, he replied, "There goes your college education."

We boarded a train for San Diego. The next three days held fantasies of exotic places; however, the moment the train stopped in San Diego, the dream state vaporized. After we were ordered to stand at attention, a Chief Petty Officer walked back and forth, before commenting, "Regardless of who you are, or how tough you think you may be, the United States Navy has a place for you. The more you screw up, the deeper the hole you dig for yourself. I strongly advise those of you with piss-poor attitudes to square yourselves away NOW! If not, you are going to have the longest and roughest four years of your lives."

Liberty was granted four times over the sixteen weeks of boot camp. Most of that time I spent at Leo Stern's gym. I could hardly wait to meet him and to train in the gym that had produced so many champions.

Leo had seen thousands of sailors like myself come and go. He invited me to look around, saying, "If you want to take a workout, it will cost you a dollar." After I

Left: Leo Stern featured on the cover of *Strength & Health* magazine in 1950, the year Leo and Bill met.

Leo Stern winning the 1946 AAU Mr. California title.

explained that I only had enough money for bus fare to get back to the training center, he remarked, "Pay me on payday."

Boot Camp was different from anything I'd experienced. Taking orders and being harassed simply because someone had the authority to do so, didn't set well. Several incidents convinced me that sixteen weeks was about all one could take. Lights-out occurred in the barracks promptly at 10:00 p.m. There was to be total silence until 4:00 a.m.; if not, everyone suffered the consequences. Someone disobeyed, which resulted in the barrack's commander ordering the platoon out of our sacks (bunks), dressed and on the grinder in double time. The next two hours were spent running in place, doing jumping jacks and push-ups. The recruit ahead of me couldn't keep up. His added punishment was having his back literally broken by being stomped on.

We normally finished classes at 4:00 p.m. Monday through Friday, which gave us time to prepare for the following day. Our clothing was washed outside, by hand, and then secured to a lanyard (clothesline) by thick pieces of string that had to be tied in square knots. Each afternoon the platoon leader would inspect the line to see if the clothing was properly hung, and clean enough to meet his satisfaction. One recruit's boxer-type undershorts failed the test. He was singled out during morning muster and then ordered to spend the rest of the day with the crotch of those shorts in his mouth, being reminded to suck out the dirt. The final eye-opener occurred during the last week of boot camp. While practicing rowing lifeboats in the bay, which separated the Naval Recruit Training Center from the Marine Recruit Training Center, we came across two bodies dressed in Marine turnouts, peacefully floating side by side. We concluded that perhaps the Navy wasn't so bad after all.

Judy, Bill, Leo and wife Bettye, back stage at the Victoria Palace, after the 1971 NABBA Mr. Universe contest.

After he graduated high school in 1939, Leo Stern opened the Hillcrest Barbell Club. He won the first Mr. San Diego title two years later. World War II erupted, and Stern served for four years as a physical training instructor in the U.S. Air Corps.

In this 1946 photo, Stern shares the camera with his new Mr. California trophy (the other, smaller trophy may be for placing third in the Mr. America contest that same year). Also in '46, Stern's Gym was established. Though it's unclear as to whether or not the 3831 Granada Avenue address is the original location, it's called "the oldest bodybuilding gym in California" by more than one online source.

— *by Robert Mizrachi*

Article about Leo Stern. Leo's gym was one of the first in California.

An early photograph of Stern's Gym in the North Park area of San Diego, California.

Chapter XIII

A WINNING NATURE

No Longer Forward

No longer forward nor behind
I look in hope or fear;
But grateful, take the good I find
The best of now and here.

John Greenleaf Whitter

Whidbey Island U.S. Naval Air Station, north of Seattle, Washington, became my home for the next two years. My job was general maintenance, working in the bowling alley or overseeing the golf driving range. Before finally being assigned to the base theater, I was sent to movie operators school to learn to run 16-millimeter projectors. Then my job was changed to driving to Seattle to pick up film, cleaning the theater and running the ticket booth and the projectors.

Prior to movie operators school (the only schooling I received during my four-year enlistment), Joe Ramirez and I had good reason to become friends. We were the lowest on the totem. If we weren't cleaning heads (toilets) or buffing floors, we alternated between working the golf driving range or the bowling alley. Just before noon on one particular day, Joe had been cutting grass while I worked the check-in counter at the bowling alley. He came running toward me with a sick look on his face, his left hand wrapped around his right. It was obvious that something had gone wrong. "What the heck happened, Joe?" I asked. "I just cut my finger off trying to dislodge a piece of wood that got stuck in the power mower!" I replied, "Bull shit!" Joe countered, "No! I really did!" I said, "Let me see."

I gently removed his left hand to pry open his clenched fist to find his index finger dangling by a thin thread of skin. Stupidly, I pulled it free with no idea what to do. A butt kit, used to dispose of cigarettes, was close. It looked convenient. I tossed his finger in with the cigarettes and then ran to the base telephone to call the infirmary. Later, a corpsman came asking, "Have any of your guys seen the finger that got cut off?"

The next day Joe was back working the bowling alley

with a huge bandage covering his hand, along with a metal splint protruding outward that held the severed finger in place, telling everyone, "If it mends, I ain't gonna' be able to move it."

We, unfortunately, slept in the same barracks, his bunk just above mine. Joe began sleeping on his stomach with his injured hand dangling about six inches from my nose. As the healing process took place, the smell was like something had died only to smell worse with time. The nightly finger dangling began causing me more pain than he was suffering. My solution was to sleep with my head at the foot of my bunk trying to keep as far away as possible from his "finger from hell." Thankfully, his hand did heal. After Joe was discharged from the Navy, he became the only licensed barber in the state of Colorado with an index finger that stuck straight out, as if giving directions to every snip of his scissors.

The weight room at the recreation center on Whidbey Island wasn't much better than what I had at home, or at the YMCA in Yakima: barbells, dumbbells, a squat rack, a home-made lat machine, a couple of flat benches and a sit-up board were scattered along the outside walls. The room also housed a boxing ring and a wrestling mat. Most weeknights the area was packed with personnel hitting speed bags, jumping rope, shadow boxing, lying around on the wrestling mat, or just gawking, which added to the confusion of those trying to get in a workout. By spending so much of my spare time in the room, I became another permanent fixture. The base newspaper had featured me in an article on weight training, which caused the role of unofficial fitness guru to fall on my shoulders.

During the two years I was stationed there, I won the Thirteenth Naval District Wrestling Championships. In

Left: One of the first photos of Pearl to appear in print. Photograph taken in 1952.

one invitational meet with the University of Washington, my opponent was slated to win that year's National Collegiate Championships. My weight training enabled me to counter most of his moves, more because of my strength than my ability. The last three minutes of our match began with the score tied at three points each. The referee started us in the down position, with the future National Champion riding me from behind. The referee hollered, "Wrestle!" I immediately went into a sit-out and then threw my body weight on his left shoulder to switch positions. During the move, I put so much pressure on that area, it caused the worst joint dislocation I'd ever seen. There was no way he could continue. Our team won the meet, while my opponent's chances of winning the Nationals went out the window.

Three-Fourths Ton of Muscle

NAVAL MATMEN—These men represented the station in wrestling matches held last Friday night against the Tacoma YM-CA. The results can be found elsewhere in this issue. From left to right and their weight division: 128, J. H. Rivard; 136, A. A. North; 145, J. C. Ramirez; 155, D. A. Stutesman, and D. R. Jones; 165, W. L. Eck; Unlimited, W. A. Pearl and R. J. Hopkins. At the far right is Z. Z. Zehenni who is managing the team under the direction of their coach LCDR Mike Lorenzo. The coach stated that to this time no one has tried out in the 121 pound class and anyone interested and eligible would be warmly welcomed.
—Official Navy Photo

The Whidbey Island U.S. Naval Air Station wrestling team. Joe Ramirez, third from the left. Bill is third from the right.

This page has been intentionally left blank.

Chapter XIV

THE MESMERIZER

At Twenty
At twenty I knew, and I knew I knew---
While at thirty, I wasn't sure.
At forty I knew that I didn't know
A lot I had known before.
At fifty I sigh, and wonder how
One who had known so much so young,
Can know so little now.

Daphne Jemmett

I had, and still have, the ability to hypnotize and to self-hypnotize. I learned the art around the age of 16. My dad had gone to school in Los Angeles, California, to become certified in hypnotherapy. When he needed a subject to practice on, his youngest son was willing. I began emulating his methods on my friends, and to my surprise, I became a better hypnotist than he. At parties or social events, someone would often mention my hypnotic talent. The usual response was, "Bet you can't hypnotize me!" That comment, or anything similar, suggests that particular individual is a prime candidate to be hypnotized. My method, back then, was to have the subject sit in a comfortable chair with his eyes focused on an object. I would begin by stressing in a slow, powerful voice, "You must zero in on what I am saying, as you begin to relax. (Pause) Let's start your relaxation with your feet and slowly work toward your head." (Pause) I would guide him through the necessary steps. "Now that you are relaxed, your eyes are becoming tired--very tired. (Pause) Your head is becoming heavier--and heavier. (Pause) Your chin wants to rest on your upper-chest. (Pause) Rest your chin on your chest. (Longer Pause) Now. As I count to ten, you will become even more relaxed and sleepier. You will feel completely safe while having no anxiety or pain. (Pause) When I reach the number ten, you will be deep...deep...deep...asleep. (Longer pause) Number one--you are becoming very sleepy." This would continue until the number ten had been reached.

Once assured that the subject was in a subconscious state, I'd lead him through a series of "whatever" to get a few laughs before I awakened him by saying, "On the count of three, you will be completely awake. Number one...you are beginning to wake up. (Pause) Number two...you are nearly awake and feeling fine. (Pause) Number three...wake up!"

Through school, practicing hypnotism was a way to have fun along with getting attention. This carried over to the recreation center at Whidbey Island U.S. Naval Air Station. I developed such terrific subjects. Some could be put into a sub-conscious state simply by telling them something like, "When I count to three...and you hear my fingers snap...you will be deep asleep."

Second Class Petty Officer George Young was one of those subjects. At one demonstration, the local civilian newspaper photographed me standing on George's mid-section with his body suspended between two chairs. His feet were on one chair and the back of his head rested on the other--nothing in between. A few of my regular subjects sat watching. Later in the demonstration, I asked them to stand and, with a specific command, they began singing silly songs and dancing around, as if having the time of their lives. A person under hypnosis will only do what they would do under normal circumstances.

Closing the demonstration, I asked if there were any questions. An officer raised his hand, "Can you help me stop smoking?" "SURE!" I said, "Come on up!" Once hypnotized I gave him the command, "From now on, every time you have the craving to smoke--the cigarette you put in your mouth will taste like crap." I then counted

Left: Self-hypnosis became a tremendous asset to Bill's bodybuilding career. "Throughout my competitive years, before each training session, I'd program myself as to what positive results would come from the workout."

to three. The officer glanced around as if he was still waiting to be hypnotized. I asked him to take out a cigarette and light it. A sick look came over him as the cigarette touched his mouth. He began licking his lips as if there was something on them that he didn't want to mention. Because of this incident, I was upgraded to the unofficial non-smoking advocate for Whidbey Island U.S. Naval Air Station.

Self-hypnosis became a tremendous asset to my bodybuilding career. Throughout my competitive years, before each training session, I'd program myself as to what positive results would come from the workout. After each meal, I'd program myself as to what I wanted the food to accomplish. At night I'd lie in bed subconsciously thinking, "I'm going to sleep and when I awake, I'll be bigger, stronger and more muscular."

Seaman's Hypnotics Poses New Possibilities

Ever have a morning when you felt like telling your leading chief to go jump into Oak Harbor? Here is a seaman who could do just that if the chief would let him do one simple thing first—hypnotize him.

Though William A. Pearl, SN of NAS Recreation has never used his talents in such manner it is quite possible that he could do just that. For visual proof of his powers look at the picture accompanying this story. It is no fake.

Taught by Father

Pearl, who joined the Navy a year and a half ago, gives credit to his father Harold F. Pearl for his instruction in hypnotism. Pearl Sr. has practiced hypnotic suggestions for 15 years as a hobbist, entertainer and sometimes for medical aid.

"It was only natural I guess," Pearl said, "that some of it should rub off on me, but I've got a long way to go before I am as good as he is."

Like any enthusiastic hobbyist Pearl was careful to explain what his field covered. Since the days of Dr. Franz Mesmer (1733-1815) and his study of this artificial sleep, mesmerism has been surrounded with fear and superstition. Many think of it being darkly related to black magic.

Pearl denounced these ideas as pure bunk. "Hypnotism can't hurt anyone, if it is properly used, and it can do a lot of good," he declared emphatically. From personal experiences he told of how his father has cured people of biting nails and heavy smoking by post-hypnotic suggestions. To do this the subject is put into a deep sleep and told that when he awakens that he will no longer smoke or bite his nails. The subject does not remember the instructions when conscious, but finds that cigarettes are bitter to him or that the idea of biting his nails is nauseating.

While this is a sensational type of hypnotism, Pearl feels that modified forms of it are used every day. "The salesman and advertisements are usually urging you to buy against your will. And what about the dentist that tells you 'this isn't going to hurt a bit'? It is my personal opinion that Hitler, Mussolini and Roosevelt were all masters of the elements of hypnotics."

Old Subjects Easiest

Pearl's method of mesmerism is to talk quietly to the subject telling him that he will become sleepy as he counts to him. With an old subject he can often have them out in five seconds as it becomes easier to hypnotize the subject each time he submits. Pearl sometimes combines his sonorous voice with a shining light to produce a pleasant eyestrain.

"The subject must want to be hypnotized," he explained "for it is impossible to do so against a person's will. An idiot or imbecile can not be hypnotized for they have no conscious mind to control."

Cannot Change Nature

According to Pearl the theory that you can make a subject perform acts that he would never do while conscious is "entirely false, a subject will never do anything against his personal code of morals and ethics while hypnotized."

Only occupational hazard involved for the hypnotist is that there is sometimes a danger, with a strong willed subject, of both of them passing out. The two of them would then stay in an artificial state of sleep for one to two hours and then lapse into normal sleep. They would awaken normally.

No person can be kept under hypnosis indefinitely and the subconscious mind would awaken the conscious mind if the body was threatened with bodily injury such as fire or flood.

Pearl does not plan to be a professional hypnotic, but said that he may be talked into performing at some of the future station talent shows. Giving a last word about his chances of hypnotizing his chief Pearl lamented, "If he would only be my subject for about five minutes I would no longer be in the division as far as he would know or care. Oh, well . . ."

For those of you that might like to know if you could be hypnotized here are a few traits that Pearl listed as making a good subject. Mind wanders (day-dreaming), walk in your sleep, and dream frequently.

"Me laughed Pearl, "I do all of them. I'm the perfect subject for a hypnotist."

You are sleepy, so sleepy . . .

HE CAN'T FEEL A THING claims William Pearl, SN of Recreation as he balances himself on top of George Young, AD2, whom he has just hypnotized. According to Pearl this is just one of the many tricks the human body can do while in a state of hypnosis. Pearl was taught by his father and has practiced hypnotics as a hobby for several years.

Bill learned the art of hypnosis around the age of 16. He would use self-hypnosis on himself for most of his bodybuilding career.

This page has been intentionally left blank.

Chapter XV

A GOLDEN OPPORTUNITY

Take a Lesson

Take a lesson to thyself,
Loving heart and true
Golden years are fleeting by,
Youth is passing, too.
Learn to make the most of life
Lose no happy day.
Time will never bring thee back
Chances swept away.

Author Unknown

All through high school I worked on the school newspaper. Eighteen months into my Navy enlistment, I decided to strike for a 3rd-class journalist rating. The rating would keep me out of mess duty and pulling night watches, while leaving a better chance of being stationed on another Naval base, or large ship, once my tour of duty at Whidbey Island U.S. Naval Air Station had ended. My concern was getting stationed onboard a small ship where weights weren't available. I took the examination, placed high on the promotion list, then bided my time waiting for an opening. The promotion came just as my tour at Whidbey Island U.S. Naval Air Station ended.

My new duty station was the Eleventh Naval District, Submarine Flotilla One, based in San Diego, California. I'd be training at Stern's Gym for the next two years.

I was assigned onboard the submarine tenders USS Sperry and USS Nereus. The tenders acted as enormous storage depots for the dozen submarines that tied up alongside. One of the two ships would anchor in the San Diego bay for six months, then rotate with the other to Hawaii for six months. There was only one billet, or job opening, for a journalist between the ships. I'd transfer from one to the other upon rotation, making sure not to leave San Diego. I didn't want anything to interfere with my training.

The Public Information Office, which I was assigned to onboard ship, consisted of a desk, two chairs, filing cabinet, wastebasket, electric typewriter and a Speed Graphic camera. My primary job was to help entertain civilian guests while at sea onboard the submarines. I would photograph them shaking hands with the ship's captain and then write a human-interest story that was sent to their hometown newspapers. Every story began the same, "Mr. X has spent the last three days as a guest of the United States Navy onboard the submarine X." The object was to get favorable publicity for the United States Navy, while showing the civilian population we appreciated their support.

The head of Public Information for the two ships was Commander William W. Williams. (A reserve officer called into active duty because of the Korean War.) Commander Williams was determined to obtain the rank of Captain before the war ended. He was the most self-centered individual I had ever met. When not entertaining civilian guests, he would order me ashore with his contemptuous attitude to run errands that seldom had anything to do with military responsibilities. One afternoon, returning from my last trip of the day, he stopped me as I entered the room, saying, "If you ever walk up to me again and don't salute, I'm going to put you on report and have your ass thrown in the brig." My response was a salute and a "Yes, Sir!" However, I promised myself that once I was out of the service I would never "salute," or "sir" anyone I didn't honestly think deserved it. If only I could meet retired William W. Williams today, my response to any of his comments would be totally different.

The only benefit of working for Commander Williams

Left: Pearl called the USS Nereus, and Stern's Gym, home for two years, while in the U.S. Navy.

Bill and training partner Vic Zanotti prepare to head up the stairs to Leo's gym.

I had taken four workouts at the gym while in boot camp. My hopes were that Leo would not only remember me, but also notice the progress I'd made during the two years while stationed at Whidbey Island U.S. Naval Air Station. To my chagrin, he didn't. What he said was, "If you want to enroll, it's going to cost you $15.00 per month, which includes instructions." In retrospect, it turned out to be one of the greatest investments of my life. The same principles he used on me were used on nearly all my members for the thirty years I was in the gym business. Leo recorded my measurements, made out a personalized training program, demonstrated the proper method to do each exercise, then ran me through the workout to make sure I understood. His closing words were, "Follow this program for six weeks. If you train regularly, then I'll make changes." I continued to keep records of how often and how long I trained, my body weight, the number of sets, reps and weight used for each exercise.

Years later, in an article written by George Coates for *Iron Man* magazine, Leo commented, "When Bill first started to work out at my gym, I didn't pay much attention to him. He was just another well-built kid who seemed to be more interested in becoming stronger to improve his wrestling. Bill was the wrestling champion for the Eleventh Naval District. He had high hopes of representing the United States in the 1952 Olympic games."

Being around Leo convinced me that the gym business was how I wanted to make a living once I was discharged from the military. When he left his gym for any reason, I took it upon myself to enroll new members, take them through workouts, pick up the weights in the gym and clean the showers. I spent most nights and weekends, when not onboard ship, on the couch in the gym's rest area. This gave me plenty of time to plan my future.

The big name at Leo's gym was Keith Stephan. He too had great hopes of becoming a champion bodybuilder. Keith was a few years older, a rugged 6-feet 2-inches tall, weighed about 240 pounds, with the looks of a budding movie star. His physique put mine to shame. We agreed to become training partners. Monday through Friday, Keith would get to the gym first and snooze on the couch. I'd climb the stairs all excited; he'd say, "You get dressed and we'll get going," or, "Yeah, you go ahead. I'll be right there." Deep inside, nothing could have pleased me more. The longer he slept and the more I trained, the better chance I had to catch him physique-wise.

was that he took every course and opportunity to help with his goal to advance in rank. Frequently, a call to his office would end by him saying, "I'll be gone from this office for the next six weeks. I expect you to carry on as if I were here." He seemed to forget that most of my time was spent running errands for him; therefore, the minute Commander Williams abandoned ship, I was right behind, not to return until the day he arrived back onboard. Though, if truth were known, anyone could have easily found me--at Stern's Gym.

Stern's was a neighborhood gym located in the North Park area of San Diego. Originally, the upper-story of the building was used as a bowling alley. The downstairs housed a poultry business that slaughtered hundreds of chickens a day. There was no pick up of garbage on weekends. On Monday mornings, it was all anyone could do to climb the stairs.

Bent-over rows was one of Bills favorite exercises.

Keith Stephan, as he appeared at the Los Angeles Greek Theater for the 1954 AAU Mr. America contest.

Chapter XVI

I KNOW WHERE I'M GOING

From the poem "Lullaby Town"
There's a quaint little place they call Lullaby Town ---
It's just back of those hills where the sunsets go down.
Its street are of silver, its buildings of gold,
And its palaces dazzling things to behold.

There's a peddler who carries, strapped high on his back,
A bundle. Now, guess what he has in that pack.
No, he's not peddling jams or delectable creams.
Would you know what he's selling?
Just wonderful dreams!

John Irving Diller

There came a time when I zeroed in on those things that would benefit me most, which meant other things had to go. Sometimes, determining what to relinquish and what to maintain isn't easy. I had won my weight division for the Eleventh Naval District Wrestling Championships the first year in San Diego. The following year, the competition was rougher. It was an Olympic-qualifying year and several of our wrestlers had an excellent chance to qualify for the United States Olympic wrestling team. That's when Leo and I began "mentally" wrestling with each other. He felt there was a real opportunity for me to succeed in bodybuilding if I focused on that alone. He told me, "Wrestling is a great sport, but you're not going to make a living at it unless you become a professional, or get a teaching credential and become a coach. You've already said that's something you don't want to do, so why waste your time on something that ends up taking you nowhere? Why not apply that energy and focus to things that you have the better chance of being successful at?"

Still, I resisted until two critical events took place. I competed in the Eleventh Naval District Wrestling Championship only to be eliminated in the first round. Weeks later, I won the AAU Mr. Southern California, and soon after, the AAU Mr. California title. My bodybuilding career had jumped into high gear. There were only a few weeks before the AAU Mr. America contest. That became

our primary goal. The members of Leo's gym got behind me by taking up a collection for my airfare to the contest, while Leo personally financed the rest of the trip.

Before the 1953 AAU Mr. America contest, Stern phoned John Grimek asking if I could train at the York

Hard work and desire were the only secrets Bill had for physical improvement.

OFFICIAL PROGRAM
1953

20c

A. A. U. SENIOR NATIONAL WEIGHTLIFTING CHAMPIONSHIP

and

"MR. AMERICA" CONTEST
June 6th and 7th

JOHN GRIMEK
York Barbell Club

*Many Physique Authorities
Claim Him to Have the Best
Physique of All Times*

Presented and Sponsored

by

**HIGGINS
HEALTH AND BODY BUILDING
GYM**

**143 East Ohio Street
Indianapolis 4, Indiana**

☆

*Under the Auspices of
The Indiana Association of the A. A. U.*

MURAT THEATER
Indianapolis, Indiana

The official program for the 1953 AAU Mr. America contest, held at the Murat Theater, in Indianapolis, Indiana.

Barbell Company's gym a week before the event. Leo wanted John to critique my posing. Leo and I thought there wasn't a chance I'd win the competition, but there was a possibility to do well in the Best-Legs, Best-Arms or Most-Muscular subdivisions.

Leo later commented in an article for *Iron Man* magazine, "Bill had fooled around with weights a lot but his serious training time, at the time he won the AAU Mr. California event, amounted to only two years, which is a relatively short period. Bill, however, surprised me by coming along, as quickly as he did. When he had first set foot in the gym, I recall him having a rugged type of physique that had possibilities, but at that time he was nothing more than a sturdy kid. He told me he had worked out at home, at the YMCA, and anywhere else he could locate weights. His main interest at that time seemed to be his wrestling, at which he was very good. He responded quickly to coaching; he was an excellent pupil. I only had to tell him once how to perform an exercise. When I outlined his programs, he followed them to the letter. It's always been a practice of mine when working with anyone that they follow the workout exactly as written, and do as instructed, or there isn't any point in coaching them. The individual who is seeking instruction shouldn't be telling the coach what has to be done."

In preparation for the AAU Mr. America contest, I spent at least two hours each day weight training, an additional two hours getting sun, plus an hour practicing posing. The trip to York, Pennsylvania, became a nightmare! My plane into Reading arrived so late my connecting flight had departed. That meant spending a sleepless night on a bench in the airport.

I became a nervous wreck wondering, "How should I treat this man? Should I call him John or Mr. Grimek?" He solved the problem, "Bill, I'm John. You're finally here. I don't suppose you've eaten. There's a good restaurant we can go to. Hear you're having trouble with your posing. What the hell is wrong with you? Anyone can hit four poses." My response was, "Leo doesn't seem to think so." He laughed, saying, "Don't worry, we'll figure out something." Years later, John commented, "It's hard to believe that Bill's posing ability wasn't much in those days. He's a master poser now, thanks to Leo's making him practice year in and year out."

The York Gym was located on the second floor of an old square brick building. Practically any gym on the West Coast would have put it to shame. So many weights had been dropped on its floor, there were holes where you could see into the packaging area below. It was a surprise to see the number of world champions training there. One of the regulars, Jim Park, (1952 AAU Mr. America), would do an exercise, and then sit on the end of a bench to smoke a cigarette.

It was also surprising how many competitors for the upcoming contest were using the facility. It was anything but inspiring. Working out in the same gym with former Mr. America winners Grimek, Park, Jules Bacon, and watching world-class lifters Steve Stanko and Tommy Kono, along with many of those I was to compete against, left me feeling depressed. Leo was correct! I knew experience was the only good coming from this ordeal.

I wasn't eating worth a darn. My $110.00 monthly Naval pay, along with the money Leo had given me, was going fast. After paying for my room at the York YMCA, I was down to living on cottage cheese, tuna fish and Hoffman's Hi-Proteen (not protein) tablets. The tablets were stored in 50-gallon drums in the York warehouse. People would walk by to snatch a handful. I figured, "What the hell." For the next five days my pockets were filled with an assortment of chocolate, vanilla and strawberry health food pills that consisted of 20 percent soybean and 80 percent refined sugar.

Leo was upset when I finally phoned. His first remarks were, "What's going on? How is the posing going? What did John decide that you should do? Are you drinking water like I told you?" I answered his last question first, "Yes, Leo, I'm drinking water." His concern was that I would dehydrate, which would cause me to lose even more muscle mass. He insisted that I carry a jug of water to constantly drink from. That's what I did. It not only helped with hydration, but also helped to wash down the hundreds of Hoffman's Hi-Proteen tablets I was eating each day.

Grimek drove his new 1953 Packard Clipper to the contest. It was easy to understand why I was his only passenger. Two of his bad driving habits were breaking the speed limit and not seeing stop signs. I spent half of the trip saying, "Oh shit! Here it comes!"

I was unnerved even more when John reached into the car's glove compartment to pull out two giant Hershey chocolate bars. "You want some chocolate?" John asked. I replied, "No, I hadn't better." "Ah, eat the damned thing. It's not going to kill you." There I sat; my eyes glued to the road, eating a two-pound chocolate bar, sipping on water with my pockets full of Hoffman's Hi-Proteen tablets, on my way to compete in the biggest contest in the sport of American bodybuilding.

We stopped for a real meal halfway to Indianapolis. A police officer eating in the restaurant recognized John and joined us. Minutes later, a beautiful blonde walked past our booth to occupy the booth behind. In a hushed voice, the officer whispered, "That blonde is the prostitute the Oleo Margarine heir got into trouble with." The scandal had made headline news. The officer went on, "He was paying her $500.00 a night for her services." John roared, "Jesus Christ, $500.00 a night! What was the guy doing, buying the broad? He could have hired a harem for that price!"

The temperature was close to one hundred degrees when we arrived in Indianapolis. The room at the downtown YMCA had two beds, no windows, or air conditioning. Everyone on that floor shared a community bath. I sat on the bed, hot, hungry, and feeling sorry for myself thinking, "If this is the real world of bodybuilding, I'm ready to head back to San Diego." There was a knock on the door. I thought it was the young man who had propositioned me in the hall. I opened the door to find Leo standing there. "Leo! What in the hell are you doing here?" He slammed the door saying, "I could tell from the phone call that you were blowing it! You blow everything

you do! Let me see the changes Grimek made in your routine." He seemed happy with the results, which put me more at ease. The prejudging was on the following day, which meant encouragement of any kind was appreciated.

Six weeks earlier I had won the AAU Mr. California title and the subdivisions for Best-Legs, for Best-Arms and for Most-Muscular. I signed up for these same subdivisions at the prejudging of the AAU Mr. America contest the following day. I not only didn't win any of these subdivisions, I wasn't called back for comparisons. It was like I hadn't been there.

Leo insisted, "You shouldn't be discouraged. It worked out fine. You're paying your dues. Next year you will do better, and the following year better yet." With those encouraging words we went to eat before spending the rest of the day in an air-conditioned movie theater.

York Barbell had sponsored the AAU National Weight Lifting Championships and the AAU Mr. America contest that year. Bob Hoffman, president of York Barbell, was a huge weightlifting fan, while he thumbed his nose at bodybuilding. The following day, the lifting began at 1:00 p.m. and finished around 9:30 p.m. The physique competitors were then called backstage, given numbers,

The 1953 AAU Mr. California contest. Dick DuBois... third, Zabo Kozewski... second and Bill... the winner.

The biggest surprise of Bill's life came when they announced he was the 1953 AAU Mr America. Pearl's first comment to Stern was, "Now, I'm really going to have to start training."

and told to be ready by the end of the thirty-minute intermission. Everyone began changing into posing trunks, doing push-ups, while trying to get someone to help apply baby oil.

We were marched on stage to form a single line. The Master of Ceremonies introduced himself to the sleepy audience, and then half-heartedly announced, "This is the lineup for the 1953 AAU Mr. America contest." Dick DuBois was the heavy favorite. Micky Hargitay, who later married movie star Jane Mansfield, had gotten tremendous publicity. Irvin "Zabo" Kozewski had high hopes. He had placed second in previous AAU Mr. America contests. Tony Sillipani, Timmy Leong and Vic Nicoletti were also favored to place high, along with Malcolm Brenner, second place winner of the last year's competition.

Posing was done under a single light that hung from a bar, center stage. Dick DuBois, the first contestant, was called out to hit a front, side, back and optional pose. As he marched off, Malcolm Brenner took his place, hitting the same three poses plus the optional pose, which was left to Malcolm's discretion. This continued until all

twenty-eight contestants had gone through their routines. We were then marched back on stage for a final look by the judges.

As we waited in the wings for the decisions, Zabo walked over, calmly saying, "Pearl, you won. DuBois is second and I'm third." I replied, "I don't appreciate your humor." He stood his ground. "I'm not kiddin'. You won!" I still didn't believe him. There was no way that I was going to win this contest! I had received the least amount of attention of any competitor. The Master of Ceremonies began announcing the top five winners. "Fifth place winner of the 1953 AAU Mr. America contest is--George Paine! (George walked out to receive his trophy.) Fourth place winner--Steve Klisanin. Third place goes to --Zabo Kozewski. Second place winner--Dick DuBois." My heart about stopped. I had either placed sixth or lower, or I HAD won the contest. "The winner of the 1953 AAU Mr. America contest is--BILL PEARL from San Diego, California!"

A six-feet four-inch beauty queen, wearing a one-piece bathing suit, stood in the middle of the stage to make the presentation. Photographers were calling for a publicity shot. Not knowing what else to do, I hoisted Miss X into my bent arms as the trophy was placed in her outstretched hands. Her derriere settled three inches off the floor as camera lights flashed. The photo appeared in newspapers throughout the country the following afternoon.

The stage filled with onlookers, as congratulations came from all sides. A feminine-looking man walked over to say in low-sensual voice, "I'm so glad you won. You don't look like the typical bodybuilder. You look more like a tennis player. I just love tennis players." I thought to myself, "That says a lot for my physique!"

Leo and I were back at the YMCA around 1:00 in the morning. All we wanted to do was sleep. A representative of Dave Garraway's <u>Today Show</u> knocked on the door with an invitation to appear that day on the show at 9:00 a.m. He had made tentative arrangements for us to leave Indianapolis at 6:00 a.m. A chauffeur-driven limousine took us to the airport where we boarded a flight to Chicago. Another limousine drove us from the Chicago O'Hare International Airport to one of the city's finest hotels, the Blackstone. A superb breakfast was served while the chauffeur waited. The TV interview lasted five minutes. It closed with Dave Garraway making flattering remarks, as I hit a couple of poses.

My world had changed overnight. The transition from staying at the YMCA in Indianapolis and worrying about money and food, to staying at the famous Blackstone Hotel in Chicago with all expenses paid, plus five hundred dollars for a five-minute guest appearance on a national television show, was cause for a drastic attitude change. I had reservations about handling all the attention, and my ability to do justice to the Mr. America title.

Finishing lunch at the Blackstone with a second piece of apple pie (my body weight had dropped from 213 pounds to 193 pounds on the day of the contest), Leo cautioned, "You've got to start conducting yourself like a champion. People are going to be looking up to you as a representative of our country. You've got to be professional about this. Stop trying to be being such a smart-ass. You're still the same fathead you've always been. And--it wouldn't hurt if you started paying back some of the positive things others have done for you."

This page has been intentionally left blank.

Chapter XVII

ONWARD AND UPWARD

Mr. Meant-To

Mr. Meant-to has a comrade,
And his name is Didn't-do.
Have you ever chanced to meet them?
Did they ever call on you?

These two fellows live together
In the house of Never-win,
And I'm told that it is haunted
By the ghost of Might-have-been

Author Unknown

Leo and my thoughts immediately turned to the NABBA Mr. Universe contest held each year in London, England. There was no other place to go. I couldn't enter the AAU Mr. America contest again and had no intentions of competing in the Mr. San Diego contest, in which I had been second runner-up six months before.

Entering the NABBA Mr. Universe was a challenge in itself. A competitor had to be invited to compete, which I was, but I also had to get special permission from the United States Navy to travel to England. Captain Ralph E. Styles, commanding officer of the USS Nereus, made the necessary military arrangements.

A month before the competition, I was flown by military air transportation to Washington, D. C., to receive special orders that assigned me to the American Embassy in London. Getting to England was a four-day ordeal. The first stop was Moffet Air Force Base, near San Francisco, then to the Aleutian Islands, and onto the Azores Islands off Portugal, before landing at a military air base outside of London.

The NABBA Mr. Universe contest was serious business. In 1952, the promoters had separated the competition into two divisions, amateur and professional. Both divisions were divided into three height classes. The winners of each height class vied for the overall amateur and professional title.

Prejudging was long and drawn out. There were

nearly 25 contestants in each of the six height classes. Each height class was judged separately. We were lined up in numerical order, then told to stand in a semi-relaxed position with our hands at our sides, feet together--and wait. Next, turn to the right, feet together--and wait; to the rear, feet together--and wait; another turn to the right, feet together--and wait; back to starting position, hands at our sides, feet together--and wait.

Once completed, each judge was given the option to call out certain contestants for comparison using the same

Jules Bacon, 1943 AAU Mr America, won his height class in the professional division of the 1953 NABBA Mr. Universe contest, while Bill won the overall amateur title.

Left: With a little more confidence but no better physique, Bill had the symmetry and proportions to win the 1953 NABBA Amateur Mr. Universe contest.

The judging panel for the 1953 NABBA Mr. Universe contest. Some of the same men sat in judgment of Pearl's physique for nearly twenty years.

procedure; to the front--and wait, to the side--and wait, to the rear--and wait, the other side--and wait, back to starting position--and wait.

Each contestant then went through a one-minute personalized posing routine before being called out again for comparisons, with each judge having the option to ask contestants to hit specific poses simultaneously. When the thirteen judges were totally satisfied, we were told to appear the following day for the finals.

The finals began at 1:00 p.m. in the London Palladium. The legendary theater buzzed with excitement. The curtains opened to a round of shouts and applause as a fifteen-piece orchestra played background music. Over one hundred twenty-five of the best physiques from around the world stood on the tiered stage, with flags from their respective countries waving in the background. Fortunately, I was positioned on the front tier, center stage. My body weight was 215 pounds and my suntan apparently made me appear more "Afro" than Native American.

The stage lighting was superb. Two spots set at slight angles overhead created excellent shadows. Additional lighting shined from the orchestra pit causing the effect of more fullness to the physiques. Back lighting created a halo, as contestants went through their routines.

My turn was coming. They had gotten to number 38 in the tall-man's amateur division. The Master of Ceremonies announced in a suave British accent, "Ladies and gentlemen... Number 38... the AAU Mr. America winner for 1953... Bill Pearl!"

I walked on stage determined to make the best possible impression. I wasn't there for more exposure or experience, but to WIN! I became the first person to capture the AAU Mr. America and the NABBA Mr. Universe titles in the same year.

The actor Sean Connery was one of the competitors in my height class in the 1953 NABBA Mr. Universe contest. While on The Tonight Show with Jay Leno, in 1999, Connery was asked about his appearance in the Mr. Universe contest. He remarked, "I was beaten by this "black" kid from the United States--Bill Pearl."

Captain Styles wanted to make certain the United States Navy received as much favorable publicity as possible from my two recent bodybuilding victories. He arranged for a special citation to be presented onboard ship. I was called out of ranks to receive the award. After handing me the presentation, he leaned forward and whispered, "Bill, get your uniform altered. Your jumper looks like there's room at the waist for two people." My reply, "Sorry, Sir. No can do, Sir. Naval regulations, Sir."

His support didn't end with the award. He arranged major television and radio interviews, had me writing fitness articles for a number of military publications, while civilian requests for articles, photos and posing exhibitions were also pouring in. Calls came to appear at grand openings and stock car races; even offers for movie roles were part of the requests. One producer suggested that I appear at several events, wearing a cape and mask. I passed by saying, "The United States Navy wouldn't approve."

My final days in the service were spent at the Coronado Naval Air Station. The day before discharge, a call came over the base intercom for all military personal to muster on the parade grounds at 14:00 hours in dress uniform. At least 2,000 gathered around a speaker's platform as the Commanding Officer stood on the podium. Looking at his watch, as if to be certain of the timing, he approached the microphone. He ordered us to form ranks on both sides of the platform before calling for parade rest. Minutes later, we were brought to attention as Military Police escorted seven men onto the parade ground. They were dressed in outlandish civilian clothing; ridiculous hats, pink and yellow shirts, ugly ties, off-colored sport coats with mis-matched trousers. One by one, their names and serial numbers were called out before announcing that they were a disgrace to the United States Navy. Each had been convicted of a felony crime. Their punishment was to be dishonorably discharged, before being handed over to civilian authorities for additional punishment. As they were handed their dishonorable discharge papers, we were again called to attention and then ordered to about face. With our backs turned, a drum roll was heard, as the seven men were marched off for further punishment.

The episode was a reminder of the comments made by the Chief Petty Officer who had met us four years earlier at the train station in downtown San Diego with advice that apparently these seven men had not heeded. "Regardless of who you are, or how tough you think you may be, the United States Navy has a place for you. The more you screw up, the deeper the hole you dig for yourself. I strongly advise those of you with piss-poor attitudes to square yourselves away NOW! If not, you are going to have the longest and roughest four years of your

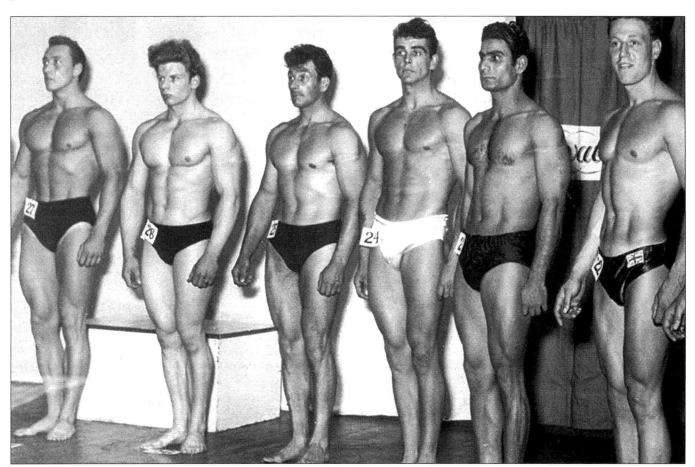

A portion of the lineup for the 1953 NABBA Mr. Universe contest. Sean Connery, number 24, became better known as "James Bond 007."

lives."

Before leaving the base, I was given additional words to consider, "You are still government property for the next 48 hours. We suggest you act accordingly."

The awards won by Bill in 1953, his first year of body building competition, ranging from the 3rd place Mr. San Diego, to the prestigious NABBA Mr. Universe trophy.

HEALTH & STRENGTH

FEB.
9
1951

1/6
Fortnightly

NATIONAL PHYSICAL FITNESS JOURNAL

Health
Culture

•

Body
Building

•

Weight
Lifting

•

Wrestling
& Judo

•

League
&
NABBA
News

The British magazine *Health & Strength* featured Bill on one of its covers. Bill was extremely popular throughout Europe.

Chapter XVIII

HONING MY SKILLS

Look Up
Look up and not down,
Look forward and not back,
Look out and not in,
Lend a hand.

Edward Everett Hale

Every few years, Leo put on The Leo Stern Variety Show in the North Park area of San Diego. The shows featured gym members, world-class weightlifters, gymnasts, hand-balancers and top bodybuilders. He'd rent a small hall, which seated around 300, and then advertise through word of mouth and posters. The events were always sellouts.

John Davis, world and Olympic heavyweight weightlifting champion, Hughie Lyons and I were the main attractions one year. Hughie's hand balancing brought the house down. He went from one astonishing balancing feat to another, finishing his act by doing a "one-finger handstand" on the base of a Coke bottle that had been turned upside down. I closed the show with a posing routine that was choreographed to music. Leo claimed this was the first time he had seen this done.

Hitting four poses to win the AAU Mr. America title with a slightly better routine for the NABBA Mr. Universe contest wasn't sufficient when it came to giving exhibitions and being paid to draw crowds. We had decided the best option was to choreograph a posing routine around music. I began by practicing to a three-minute version of the very powerful theme song, "Exodus." Leo helped with the selection of the thirty poses necessary to fill the time. He took photographs to make sure each pose was what we wanted. I scrutinized the photos, the position of my head, hands and feet, as well as the overall symmetry of each pose. We then arranged the photos on a large piece of cardboard. I practiced each position in sequence until it became second nature to know when to transition from one to the other, as it corresponded to the music.

Posing remained an intricate part of my bodybuilding

career. It not only kept me focused, but enabled me to broaden my ability to impact an audience by coming up with innovative routines. It wasn't long before other bodybuilders followed suit. Choreographed posing routines eventually became a standard part of the sport of bodybuilding.

Leo and I had become a team. For the next twenty-five years, to the bodybuilding world our names were synonymous--Pearl and Stern. We both had specific jobs that one could do better than the other. His job was taking care of details, mine was to be in shape and perform like a professional. He continually stressed the importance of staying in the public's eye, by subscribing to the saying, "If you are out of sight, you are out of mind." He felt I had the ability to make a long-term impact only if I could stay current through two or three generations of the sport. By winning the most prestigious bodybuilding contest every four or five years and giving exhibitions throughout the world for another fifteen, I was able to stay near the top through four generations of the sport.

Stern wasn't, and still isn't, known for passing out compliments. Don Farnsworth, my long-time friend and training partner, was complaining about a shoulder injury. I said, "Call Leo. He's the smartest person I know when it comes to rehabilitating injuries. He'll be happy to help you." Don shook his head and replied, "You've got to be kidding! He's not going to help me, or anyone else. You're the last person Leo's ever befriended."

Another example of Leo's candor surfaced years ago while in Columbus, Ohio, after we had finished judging the Arnold Classic. A contestant staying at our hotel got on the elevator and immediately asked, "Leo, what the heck happened?" Apparently he felt he hadn't placed as

Left: By the mid 1950s, posing had become an intricate part of Pearl's bodybuilding career.

VALDON

Hughie Lyons preforming a sample of his amazing acrobatic feats that he used for <u>The Leo Stern Variety Show</u>.

high in the contest as he had expected. Leo casually replied, "Well--you somehow made your way to Columbus, Ohio. You entered a physique contest and looked like shit. Now--you're in an elevator. I'll let you take it from there."

Fortunately, I could always count on Leo. We had agreed to do an exhibition in a rough section of Brooklyn, New York, in the mid 1960s. Leo insisted that I have privacy before I went on stage. The promoter stuck me on the top floor of this one-hundred-year-old theater in a dirty, empty room, with two chairs and a light hanging from a frayed cord.

The audience became impatient when the event was an hour late in getting started. Halfway through the preliminaries, the crowd was throwing objects at the contestants. Sitting in the dingy room for over two hours, I could hear the tension mounting. Leo finally came to say, "You got about thirty minutes before going on." I

confided, "I have a premonition that I'm going to be shot and killed." I wasn't kidding. The audience had become so hostile that it worried me going on stage. Seeing how upset I had become, Leo paced the floor before speaking, "We can do one of two things. You can either refuse to go on or, when I do the introductions, I'll tell those assholes if they have ideas about taking their frustrations out on you, they're going to have to go through me." Leo made the announcement. I went on stage and brought the house down.

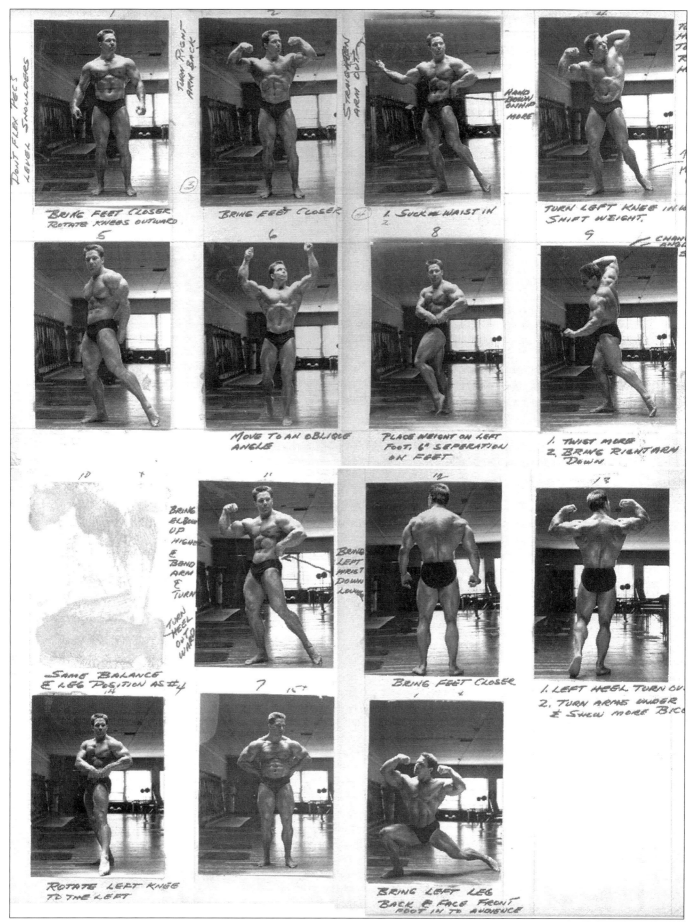

Bill and Leo used photography to design the posing routines he used during his nearly 20-year career as a bodybuilder. Leo would shoot the poses and mount them on a large piece of cardboard with suggestions as to how each pose should be hit. It was Bill's job to practice and choreograph the routines to music.

Chapter XIX

MY HEROES HAVE ALWAYS BEEN IRONMEN

'Advice'
Take the open air,
The more you take the better;
Follow Nature's laws
To the very letter.
Let the doctors go
To the Bay of Bicay,
Let alone the gin,
The brandy, and the whiskey.
Freely exercise,
Keep your spirits cheerful;
Let no dread of sickness
Make you ever fearful.
Eat the simplest food,
Drink the pure, cold water,
Then you will be well,
Or at least you oughter.

Author Unknown

Of all the physique stars I've admired, John Grimek and Friederick Muller topped my list. Friederick Muller was better known by his stage name, Eugen Sandow. At the turn of the 20th Century, he was the person most responsible for bringing physical fitness to the forefront throughout the world. He was born in East Prussia (Germany), in 1867, and began his professional career as a wrestler/strongman at the age of 18. He stood 5' 9" tall, weighed 190 pounds, while being touted as the strongest man in the world pound for pound.

Sandow performed in most major theaters throughout Europe before visiting the United States. In 1893, he met Florenz Ziegfeld at the Chicago's World's Fair, where he helped judge the first physique contest held in this country. Sandow gave a special posing demonstration so impressive that it surpassed anything seen in the United States. He also demonstrated a series of amazing feats, such as supporting 4,000 pounds on his shoulders. Ziegfeld was so impressed, he signed Sandow to a long-term contract with the Ziegfeld Follies, paying him $3,500.00 per week. Sandow became an instant star. Everything masculine had his endorsement: Sandow Cigars, Sandow Cigarettes and Sandow Chewing Tobacco. Nearly every tonsorial parlor (barbershop) in the country had a photo of Sandow hanging on their walls to help sell moustache-wax.

Sandow moved to England in 1910, married, and fathered two daughters. His wife became increasingly jealous of his ever-growing popularity. To appease her, he stopped making stage appearances. He opened health clubs in some of the major cities in England and wrote several books on weight training, while also designing special fitness courses for the British military.

His domestic downfall came when he allowed the Royal Society of Natural History to cast his body in plaster as a part of an exhibition on the New Theory of

Left: Eugen Sandow began his professional career as a wrestler/strongman at the age of 18. He stood 5' 9" tall and weighed 190 pounds. Some considered him the strongest man in the world--pound for pound.

Sandow supports the Trocadero Company, with Florenz Ziegfeld sitting above his head, on December 21, 1895. The total weight was reportedly close to 4,000 pounds.

Evolution by Darwin. The finished, life-sized statue presented him completely nude, which disgraced his prudish wife and ended their marriage.

He died in 1925, at the age of fifty-eight, reportedly after lifting the back of a large automobile while a friend changed a tire. Sandow supposedly lowered the car, then dropped dead from a brain hemorrhage. The story goes that his ex-wife discovered there were two showgirls in the car at the time of the accident. She became so irate that she buried his remains in an unmarked grave, then spent the rest of her life, and most of his money, collecting all the memorabilia she could find on him, only to destroy it. What is known for certain is that Sandow was buried in an unmarked grave.

In the mid-1930s, John Fritze opened a health club in a part of Philadelphia, Pennsylvania, called German Town. John Fritze was part of the clan of old-time bodybuilders and strongmen, from the 1910s through the 1930s, that Leo and I greatly admired. When I was asked to be a part of his annual Physique Extravaganza, we decided to pattern one of my posing routines after a routine preformed by Eugen Sandow at the World's Fair in Chicago, Illinois, in 1893.

Growing up as a fan of Sandow, I had acquired memorabilia on him from collectors around the world including India, New Zealand, Australia, England, the United States, Canada and Germany. Several dozen photos and film footage taken by Thomas Edison showing his posing routine, as well as every book and exercise chart Sandow had written, are included in my collection.

We did our best to keep the Sandow routine as authentic as possible by not adding or subtracting from what photos or the film showed. This was more difficult than it sounds. Sandow posed exactly opposite from the way bodybuilders do today. If his stomach protruded from his swayback positioning--that's what I practiced. If one of his legs was planted like a tree stump--that's what I did.

For more authenticity, my posing briefs were made of bearskin, and from a novelty/costume store in New York City, we ordered roman sandals, a fake moustache, along with a tin of white body powder to cover my body to give a ghost-like appearance.

All of this was emphasized by the black, box-like enclosure we had built, just large enough to maneuver from one pose to the next. We decided that rather than having a single overhead light, we'd use a series of controllable small strobe lights and mini-spots, which allowed Leo to accent my physique from different angles.

On the day of the exhibition, we were at the auditorium hours before opening to set up special overhead lights, mini-spots and props. When it was time to appear on stage, Leo took charge of the microphone and the house lights. He dimmed the theater until nearly dark before priming the audience. His voice thundered over the microphone, "Ladies and gentlemen--you are about to see a man with a true 20-1/2 inch muscular arm at a body weight of 222 pounds." Leo hit the mini-spot that focused on my left arm, as I banged out an arm shot. "Now you are about to see a set of legs that have officially squatted over 600 pounds." Two mini-spots became focused on my thighs, as I flexed them. He continued the buildup from one muscle group to the next and finished by saying, "NOW--the man who is acclaimed to have the greatest physique in the world today--Bill Pearl!"

As the special overhead lighting covering my small portion of the stage began to glow, I stood statuesque for several seconds before the sound of "Exodus" was heard. A few bars into the music, my routine began. I held each pose for a count of six to eight beats, with four counts to transition from one pose to the next. Minutes later, the music ended with me hitting what we called the "Statue-of-Liberty" pose. As the house lights rose and the overheads faded, I bowed to the audience and hurried offstage to get ready for the Sandow routine.

Leo again set the scene. "You are about to see a special event to honor the past greats who have made bodybuilding what it is today. Bill in going to emulate a posing routine performed by Eugen Sandow, at the World's Fair in Chicago, Illinois, in 1893."

The curtains opened with me standing in the boxed enclosure, my arms crossed over my chest, and my chin sticking out like Benito Mussolini's. Nickelodeon-type music began to play as small spotlights flicked on and off, causing my movements to emulate a "Keystone Cop" movie.

The applause grew as the routine progressed and ended with me standing, as I had begun--my arms crossed over my chest, but this time with a huge smile on my face. Listening to the crowd's reaction, I remembered myself as that ten-year-old kid standing in the front yard, watching the strongman on the back of the elephant,

"Sandow the Magnificent" (in tuxedo on left) judging the first physique contest held in the U.S. in the year 1893.

thinking, "That's exactly what I want to do with my life!" Hard work, plus years of dedication, had paid off.

John Grimek, my second all-time hero, was featured on the cover of the first physique magazine I had purchased. The photograph remains ingrained in my memory, as if it were yesterday. From the eighth grade on, when writing about someone I admired, John always got the nod. He was born in Perth Amboy, New Jersey, in 1910, and became the World's Best-Built Man and the World's Most-Muscular Man of his time. He was admired throughout the world, much like his predecessor, Eugen Sandow.

Not considered a full-time strongman, Grimek performed many impressive feats of strength, which included lifting heavy weights, bending bars and spikes and hitting a thick iron poker across his forearm until it bent. He was the AAU American Weightlifting Champion of 1936, and several times North American champion. He also achieved the highest total of any American weightlifter at the Berlin Olympic Games of 1936. A few years before he died, John mentioned to me that he had

Formal portrait of Sandow dignifying himself as an Edwardian businessman.

shaken Adolph Hitler's hand just after receiving his medal.

John won the AAU Mr. America title in 1940 and again in 1941. Then a ruling was passed making it impossible for anyone to win the contest more than once. He went on to win the first Mr. Universe contest held in 1948 and the first Mr. USA title in 1949.

Grimek and I appeared on the same stage at the annual Ed Yarick Show held in Oakland, California, in 1954. The event was based around a variety-show format: fourteen acts, consisting of bodybuilding, weightlifting and hand balancing. Former world heavyweight boxing champion Max Baer acted as Master of Ceremonies. The show opened with my posing routine and closed with John's routine of muscle control and posing. I was seated next to Clancy Ross (AAU Mr. America of 1945) when Grimek came on stage. I asked Clancy, "What do you think of Grimek's physique?" His comment, "He looks good for a midget! But there is no room in this game for midgets!" (Clancy and John had their differences over the years.)

The Ed Yarick Show of 1954 was John's final public posing exhibition. For the next several years, he turned over all the requests for appearances to me. He was responsible for my trip around the world, to India, Mexico, England, etc.

We corresponded regularly for the next forty years, with John always replying on the back of the letter I had written him. When my travels took me near York, Pennsylvania, I'd either phone or stop by. When he made trips to southern California, he reciprocated.

John visited our Pasadena Health Club in the mid-1970s and gave some excellent advice in the form of a comment. One of the members asked, "John, how long have you been training?" John replied, "I've trained regularly for the past fifty years." The member's mouth dropped before replying, "Man! Why so long?" John blurted out, "What the hell! I had to live that long!"

In the late 1990s, I was still learning from John. He remarked that his right hip was causing such pain that for the past few years he was only riding a stationary bicycle. Thinking back on John's career, with the importance weight training had had in his life, I decided in this instance not to follow in John's footsteps. Regardless of my injuries, I started out lifting weights--I would go out lifting weights. My final lesson learned from John came on the night he passed away: even the likes of the great John Grimek have to face the inevitable.

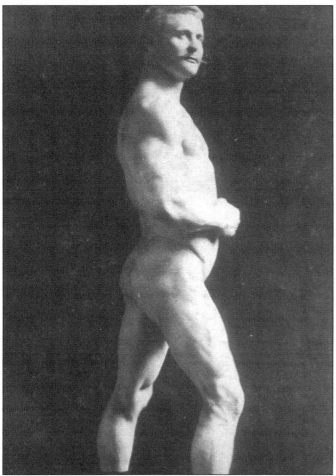

Three photographs of Eugen Sandow, in the year 1893, proudly posed with the aid of a fig leaf at the Chicago World's Fair.

On this page and the next page, you will see Bill emulating portion of a posing routine of his childhood idol, Eugen Sandow.

Three photographs of John Grimek. He was admired throughout the world, much like his predecessor, Eugen Sandow.

Grimek and Pearl appeared on the same stage at the annual <u>Ed Yarick Show</u> held in Oakland, California, in 1954. The best seats in the theater sold for $2.40.

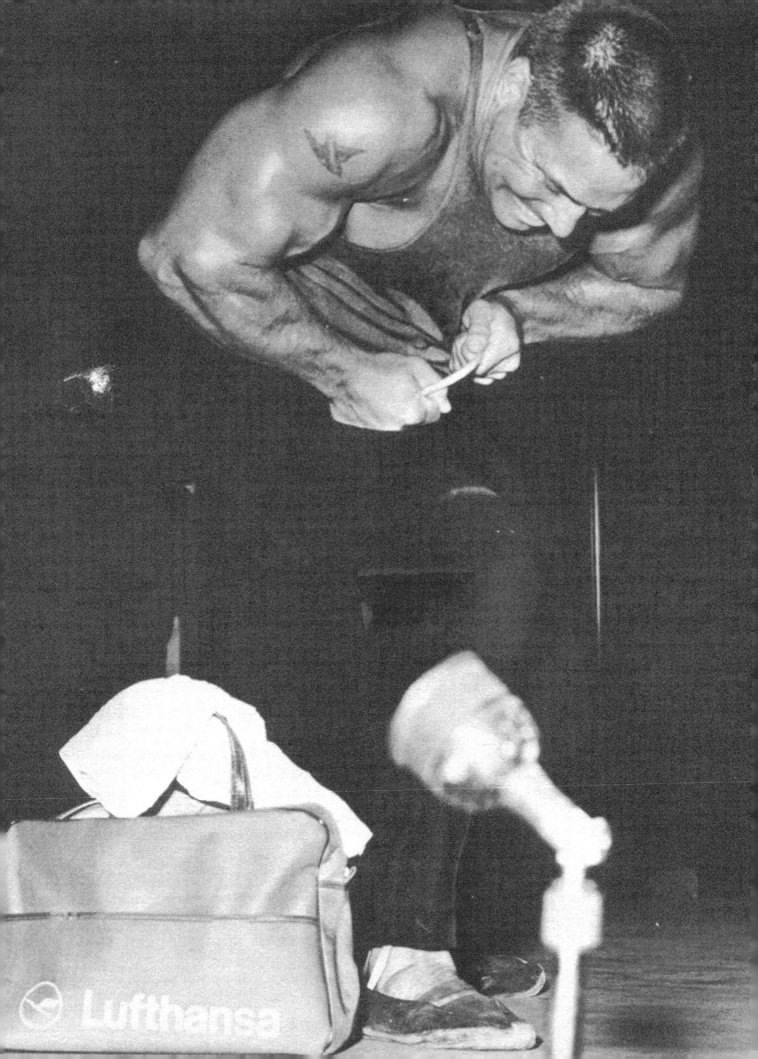

Chapter XX

FANS, YOU 'GOTTA' LOVE 'EM!

If I Were A Voice
If I were a voice, a persuasive voice,
That could travel the wide world through,
I would fly on the beams of the morning light,
And speak to men with a gentle might,
And tell them to be true.

I'd fly o'er land and sea,
Wherever a human heart might be,
Telling a tale, or singing a song,
In praise of the Right and in blame of the Wrong.

Charles Mackay

From the beginning of my weightlifting career, I took pride in the fact that I had practiced many of the feats that old-time strongmen were noted for. I attributed a lot of my added strength to those basic movements. In my prime, performing a seated press-behind-neck with 300 pounds, curling 100-pound dumbbells, doing palms-up wrist curls with 185 pounds, front squatting 500 pounds, and doing regular squats with 600 pounds--without the aid of wraps, belts, or a lifting suit... was part of my regular training.

However, when being paid to draw crowds, executing lifts that were close to my limit was not something I could do with assurance of success. I began to practice bursting hot water bottles, breaking chains, tearing auto license plates, bending horseshoes and tent spikes mainly because these items could easily be carried on tour; and with consistent practice there was less chance for failure.

Why did I add feats of strength to my more important presentations? Mostly, for additional respect and recognition. It also helped separate my exhibitions from other contemporary bodybuilders' by making it harder for them to duplicate what I was doing.

Many of the old-time strongmen were having difficulty accepting the current crop of bodybuilders. It seemed more emphasis was being placed on developing physiques that looked good on the beach, rather than on

strength, or the benefits derived from weight training.

The old-timers viewed the younger generation of bodybuilders as opportunists who were using the sport as a steppingstone to get into movies and live stage, or as a way of being kept. There were exceptions: Chuck Sipes, Sergio Oliva, Marvin Eder and Bill Seno. These, and several others, could hold their own against anyone.

I was another who had a different attitude than many

Tearing a matching pair of automobile license plates was a small part of Bill's feats of strength.

Left: "Driving a 70-penny tent spike through your hand isn't a fun thing to do!"

Harold Morrison, M.D., holds his hands over Pearl's eyes for protection, as Bill blows up and bursts a hot water bottle during a Rockwell International executive luncheon.

of the bodybuilders of that era. Reading about Eugen Sandow, Louis Cyr, Siegmund Klein, George F. Jowett and John Grimek, while knowing that weight training had a history thousands of years old, which dated back to when ancient warriors used it as a system for survival, I wanted to show the old-time strength athletes the respect I felt they deserved.

When I began practicing feats of strength, bending a 60-penny nail was relatively easy. It is something that most people who use their forearms, wrists, and hands for heavy work can accomplish. I'd wrap the nail in a washcloth, place both hands around it, and then press down hard until my knuckles touched, before interlocking my fingers and squeezing.

It took months of practice before I could master the 70-penny tent spike. The difference between the two is like comparing a mini-van to an SUV. A 60-penny nail is about the size of a lead pencil while a 70-penny tent spike is nearly twelve inches long and easily twice as thick.

I vividly recall the first 70-penny tent spike I bent. Using the same grip as on the 60-penny nail, I drove down with all my physical strength to the point where nothing was left, and then I mentally went one step further-- PRESTO. This proved to me that although I'd always had the physical strength, I hadn't been pushing myself hard enough mentally. Once knowing it was possible, I became a specialist.

However, being a specialist doesn't mean you always succeed. Leo and I were finishing a two-week tour along the Eastern seaboard of the United States. Our last stop was Louisville, Kentucky. I was bending a spike when it slipped, which caused the sharp end to go through the palm of my left hand, coming out the backside. Raising my arm to show the audience what had happened, they apparently thought it was part of the act. The applause began as blood flowed. Leo stood watching from the wings as I yelled, "We've got a problem." He walked on stage; "What the hell did you do, run it through your hand?" "Yeah!" I said. "Pull the damn thing out!" He grabbed, pulled, but nothing happened. It took two stagehands, plus Leo, tugging like mad, to extract it.

Returning to my dressing room with my hand twice its normal size, we found this burly young man waiting at the dressing room door. He had traveled three-hundred miles to challenge me to an arm wrestling contest for $500.00. I looked at him, turned to Leo and said, "That's your department. You take care of it." It took days before I could close my hand, and months before I was back to bending spikes.

Chapter XXI

NOT JUST ANOTHER PRETTY FACE

When Life Seems Just A Dreary Grind
When life seems just a dreary grind,
And things seem fated to annoy,
Say something nice to someone else.
And watch the world light up with joy.

Author Unknown

From the 1940s to the mid-1970s, contests of the American Athletic Union, (AAU), and the National Amateur Bodybuilding Association, (NABBA), were considered the epitome of physique contests. The AAU was not exclusively a bodybuilding organization; it sponsored all types of athletic competitions from swimming to track and field. Owning the Mr. America title placed the AAU in a league of its own. The same applied to the NABBA Mr. Universe title. Winning either title had the prestige that winning the IFBB Mr. Olympia contest has today. The first IFBB Mr. Olympia contest was held in 1965. It was the brainchild of Joe and Ben Weider. They formed the IFBB in 1947 to compete against the AAU and the NABBA Recognition of the Weider's organization was helped by the release of the movie Pumping Iron in 1977. The movie featured many of the IFBB Mr. Olympia competitors, Arnold Schwarzenegger, in particular. Arnold's stepping onto the scene in the mid-1960s had one of the most profound impacts on the sport since the reign of Eugen Sandow and John Grimek. The more coverage the IFBB received, the higher the jackpots grew. Money was the big incentive for more of the top bodybuilders to cross over to the IFBB Neither the AAU nor the NABBA awarded cash prizes. Once the big purses were offered, a whole new attitude began to emerge in the sport.

Although the AAU Mr. America had a prestigious reputation that set it apart from other amateur competitions, it was not without screw ups.

In the mid-1960s, the AAU Physique committee began to employ a new point system, based on factors other than the contestants' physique. Much like what happens in Miss America contests, they were looking for articulate, well-rounded individuals, who if called upon, could represent the sport at the highest level. Anything to prove the contestant was more than just a physique!

This lasted approximately five years before being abandoned. To say the interviews got out of hand is putting it mildly. Contestants were showing up at prejudging in tailor-made suits, shoes shined and nails manicured. Others carried diplomas, scrapbooks and "To-Whom-it-May-Concern letters" hoping to impress the judges.

The scoring system put some top competitors at a definite disadvantage. Harold Poole (runner up in the 1962 and 1963 AAU Mr. America contests) had the ideal physique to represent the sport at its highest level. The problem was that Harold was black and he stuttered badly. The judges' thoughts were, "God forbid if he were asked to represent the sport as a public speaker."

Mel Williamson was another of the many contestants to become disenchanted with the interview system. Mel felt competitors should be judged on their physique, posing ability and overall appearance. Much like Harold Poole, he had a lot going for him. He had a terrific physique, with a chest so thick you could balance a cup and saucer on his upper pectorals. He was also a brilliant young man, who worked as a biochemist for the Dole Pineapple Corporation. He later produced the MLO

Left: During the mid-1960s, several bodybuilding contestants became disenchanted with the system that the AAU was using to judge physique contests.

Harold Poole, winner of the 1963 IFBB Mr. Universe and the 1964 IFBB Mr. America titles.

health food line, which is still sold throughout the world.

His frustrations over being interviewed grew when at one particular contest the judges seemed more concerned about his athletic abilities than his physique. When questioned, he informed them that he was an expert archer with the abilities of the legendary William Tell. To prove this, he had brought his bow and arrows with the idea of shooting apples off their heads. Mel didn't win the contest, yet, seemed content with second place until one of the judges insisted on trying to console him by saying, "If it wasn't for your enormous handlebar moustache, you could have won the contest easily. I'm sure you'll win the

next one, if you just cut it back." Mel took the judge's advice by entering the next contest with the right side of his moustache completely gone and the left side sticking out in all its glory.

The sport has many such odd, humorous and sometimes disillusioning incidents in its history.

In the late 1960s, for instance, Tommy Kono (possibly the greatest Olympic weightlifter the United States has ever produced) competed in the National Championships in San Jose, California. Tommy had represented York Barbell for several years. When he failed to win his weight class that year, York refused to pay his way back to Hawaii. The audience took up a collection for his return airfare.

Another example was when Larry Scott (former IFBB Mr. America, IFBB Mr. Universe and two-time IFBB Mr. Olympia winner) decided to enter the Diamond Cup physique championships held in Vancouver, British Columbia, in 1978. Acting as Master of Ceremonies, I made it a point to give Larry a tremendous build-up prior to his coming on stage. I failed to mention that Larry hadn't competed since winning his last Mr. Olympia title in 1966. When the head judge announced the top five competitors, Larry's name wasn't called. I asked him how it felt; he replied, "This is a very humbling experience. I believe people would rather remember me as I was, and not as I am."

Tommy Kono, possibly the greatest Olympic weightlifter the United States has ever produced.

Here's one on me. Judy and I were home relaxing in our bathrobes having a cup of coffee one Sunday morning. There was a knock on the door. The greeting came from a stranger dressed in Levis and a form fitting T-shirt, with his fat belly hanging over his belt, "Are you Bill Pearl?" I said, "Yeah." After a long moment of silence he asked, "What the hell happened to you?" Trying to remain friendly, my response was, "Nothing has happened to me. The way I look is the way I look. Nobody can live what the magazines portray twenty-four hours a day." He responded by shaking his head, saying, "I drove all the way from New York for this? What a bunch of shit!" Needless to say, we didn't invite him in for coffee.

Larry Scott, winner of the 1965-1966 IFBB Mr. Olympia titles, has remained an icon in the sport.

All work and no play made Bill a dull boy.

Chapter XXII

WHERE ARE THE CLOWNS?

Judged By The Company One Keeps

One night in late October,
When I was far from sober,
Returning with my load with manly pride,
My feet began to stutter,
So I lay down in the gutter,
And a pig came near and lay down by my side:
A lady passing by was heard to say:
"You can tell a man who boozes,
By the company he chooses,"
And the pig got up and slowly walked away.

Author Unknown

Bert Goodrich, winner of the 1939 AAU Mr. America title in New York (Roland Essmaker also won a Mr. America contest held in Chicago, Illinois that same year), was the promoter of the Professional Mr. USA contest. The show was always a huge success. It attracted the top thirty-five or forty physiques in the country, while drawing five thousand to seven thousand spectators. Part of the lure of the competition was that each first-place winner received a $1,000.00 cash prize. The 1956 USA was no exception. The lineup turned out to be the "Who's Who" of the top American bodybuilders. Clarence Ross was my biggest concern. With Grimek's retirement, Clancy had become the man to beat. Another concern was that he and Leo were best friends. They'd served together in the United States Army Air Corps, during World War II. Leo had coached him as he rose to fame in 1945 by becoming the youngest to win the AAU Mr. America title. I felt this put Leo in an awkward position because of his loyalty toward both of us. My concern was that if I did win the contest, it might have a bearing on their friendship. That was not the case. Clancy took the defeat with a smile. His response was, "I've had a good run. Youth must be served."

The following evening, Bert Goodrich invited Leo, his wife Bettye, Leo's seventy-five-year-old mother, my first wife, Sylvia, and me, to be his guests at a plush restaurant/night club in Hollywood. I assumed this was part of settling our account.

Mr. and Mrs. Goodrich, along with a dozen others, were seated at a long table when we arrived. Without any introductions, Mrs. Goodrich pointed toward the far end, saying, "Leave space in between our groups. We're expecting four more." Without reservation, I "diplomatically" replied, "Where's my $1,000.00?" Bert dug into his pocket to hand me a check for $500.00, explaining, "I gave the other $500.00 to the second and third place winners." Not wanting to cause problems, I took a seat as Bert's press agent stomped on stage to announce that, "Bert Goodrich, our first Mr. America winner, and Bill Pearl, the winner of last night's Mr. USA contest, have just arrived. Please come up." We stumbled up the ramp with little acknowledgment from the patrons. The press agent looked at me like I was supposed to perform a miracle to get everyone's attention. Bert finally broke the silence by saying, " Bill! Do something! Take off *your* shirt and pose!" I turned to walk offstage saying, "You're a former Mr. America winner. Take *your* shirt off and pose."

A waiter came to inquire about drinks. Bert's wife blurted out, "Don't bother with them at the other end. They're a bunch of health nuts." Thirty minutes later, he was back to take food orders. One of their guests asked, "Hey Bert! Who's picking up the check?" Mrs. Goodrich shouted, "If Pearl thinks Bert's going to pick up the tab

Left: Bill winning the 1956 Mr. USA contest.

after the stunt he pulled, he's full of crap." That was it! I was out of my chair heading their way. As the press agent jumped up to protect them, I retaliated by grabbing and shoving him around while the rest of their party stayed seated. Mrs. Goodrich screamed, "Help! Help! He's a mad man!" I was ushered out of the restaurant as Leo's mother sat laughing, and clapping her hands, as if having the greatest time of her life.

Clancy Ross, winner of the 1945 AAU Mr. America contest. Clancy was also coached by Leo Stern.

Clancy Ross commented to Bill after the 1956 Mr. USA contest, "I've had a good run. Youth must be served."

Official program for the 1956 AAU Mr. and Miss USA contest and pageant.

Chapter XXIII

BEST LAID PLANS

The Optimist
The optimist fell ten stories,
At each window bar
He shouted to his friends:
"All right so far."

Author Unknown

I had committed to appear at Mitts Kowashima's Mr. Hawaii contest, two weeks after winning the Mr. USA contest. I had also committed to Sylvia to have a vasectomy before leaving for Hawaii. We were married in 1954 and by 1956 were blessed with two children, Kimberly and Philip, with our third, Reneé, on the way. With plans for a long marriage, our concern was that the blessings would continue unless something drastic took place. My plan was to have the operation on Thursday, travel to Hawaii on Friday, do the exhibition on Saturday, and then spend three days on the beach relaxing. The doctor explained the procedure as, "There's nothing to it. I'll do it in my office. It won't take more than thirty minutes. If you'll take it easy for a few days you'll be as good as new."

I got to the doctor's office on time. His very young nurse pointed to a small operating room, saying, "Undress and put on a hospital gown." She knocked before entering and began pulling instruments from a sterilizer. Glancing my way she remarked, "You haven't shaved!" Rubbing my chin, I replied, "Yes I have. I shaved this morning." Pointing at my crotch, she said, "You haven't shaved. Lie on the table."

The doctor arrived in great spirits. By now, his first patient of the day was anxious for him to get started. He donned a smock, washed his hands while his nurse waited to help with the rubber gloves.

He reached for a huge syringe, raised it to eye level then began squeezing the plunger to remove bubbles, I said, "Where're you going to stick that needle? I hate needles!" There was no need for reply. The nurse graciously assisted as he pulled my testicles to an all time high, saying, "You'll feel a few little pricks." Twenty minutes later, my ability to reproduce had ended.

But, all is NOT well that ends well. As with the lack of communication about shaving, nothing had been mentioned about transportation. I'd ridden my bicycle to the gym and then rode the couple of miles to the doctor's office. It was time to ride the couple of miles back. Upon arriving at the gym, I felt a slight discomfort and decided to investigate. A quick peek revealed my testicles were the

Bill and his first wife, Sylvia.

Left: A photo of Bill, as he prepared to guest pose for the 1956 Mr. Hawaii contest.

size of grapefruit! My first thought was to call Mitts and let him know his guest poser had contracted elephantiasis. Instead, I talked myself into believing things would be back to normal by Saturday. When it was time to go on stage, there wasn't room in my posing briefs for one testicle, let alone two. It looked like someone had stuffed a pair of socks--along with everything else, into the confined area.

The contest was a sellout, as usual. After a tremendous introduction, I faced the audience with my hands crossed over the front of my trunks. As the stage lights grew brighter and brighter I hit my first pose. The only response was a loud gasp. My second pose--another gasp. This went on pose after pose--no clapping or words of encouragement, just gasps. Halfway through the routine, the gasps had convinced me that my testicles were stealing the show. As the music faded, I stood waiting for the applause that never came. There was

complete silence. I felt like hell. Mitts stood silently in the wings, as I walked over to say, "I'm so sorry, Mitts! I laid a giant egg. I apologize." He replied, "Laid an egg! You're kidding! You were terrific! We've never seen anyone with that kind of size before." To this day, I still wonder which size he was talking about; the size of my arms or the size of my "you know whats!"

Bill with his youngest daughter, Reneé, son, Philip, first wife, Sylvia, and daughter, Kimberly.

This page has been intentionally left blank.

Chapter XXIV
ACCOLADES

Charity

There is so much good in the worst of us,
And so much bad in the best of us,
That it ill behooves any of us
To find fault with the rest of us.

Author Unknown

I won the 1961 NABBA Professional Mr. Universe contest by taking every first place vote. George Coates, contributing editor for *Iron Man* magazine, wrote the following: "Bill Pearl has charisma that not many people can match. I can remember being at the judging of the 1961 NABBA Mr. Universe Contest. I swear a lot of the contestants could hardly concentrate on their own posing, as all eyes were riveted on Pearl. John Grimek was a great attraction and had tremendous stage presentation. Steve Reeves during his short run as a contestant, also seemed to have great crowd appeal. Reg Park and Clancy Ross were big crowd pleasers along with a few others, but when Bill Pearl appears at a show, as a contestant or guest poser, there appears to be an atmosphere unlike any other I've seen. It's almost as if the whole show revolves around this one man. "Can he be as fantastic as his pictures," seems to be the most repeated question. Bill Pearl never disappoints them! Most people can only gasp and shake their heads in disbelief at first sight of Pearl. Even the old hands who have seen him many times always end up by remarking, "He's even greater than he was last time."

George Coates, Leo Stern and Bill have remained close friends for over 50 years.

Left: Bill's physique grew more mature as the years passed. He was now setting the highest standards. For the 1961 NABBA Professional Mr. Universe, the judging was 100% in Pearl's favor.

Chapter XXV

EAST IS EAST AND WEST IS WEST

The Ballad of East and West
Oh, East is East, and West is West,
And Never the twain shall meet,
'Till earth and sky stand presently
At God's great judgment seat,
But neither East nor West,
Border, nor breed, nor birth,
When two strong men stand face to face,
Though they come from the ends of the earth!

Rudyard Kipling

By 1966, I was giving exhibitions as much overseas as in the United States, traveling throughout Europe, Mexico, Canada, the Far East and South Africa. One of my most memorable trips took me around the world. A top executive of a large industrial conglomerate in Bombay, India, had invited Grimek to visit his country. John declined with the recommendation that I take his place.

Landing in Bombay late at night, it was still deathly hot. It remained that way for the three-week tour. Going through customs was just a preview of the unique experiences ahead. The building reeked of odd smells, while people slept everywhere. It was impossible to walk without stepping on, or over, someone. Rhanjana Byjar, a former Miss India, was waiting for me. She had been assigned as my guide and travel companion.

My suite at the Bombay Cricket Club, in downtown New Delhi, had no cooling system, except for an oscillating fan. The room was just large enough for a bed, dresser, closet and toilet. Every time the shower was used, cockroaches erupted from the drain to cover the floor. Eating in the club's dining room was another experience. My assigned waiter wore nothing but sandals, a loincloth and turban. One of his not-so-endearing habits was to remove a filthy towel from the front of his loincloth, wipe the tabletop, plates and chair, and then stand back to scratch his crotch. In an effort to achieve some sort of

hygiene, I would go into the kitchen, have the chef throw a piece of water buffalo on the grill to cook until crisp, and

Dennis Tinerino, 1967 AAU Mr. America, Bill, and Craig Whitehead, M.D., third place 1963 AAU Mr. America, do their best to make their mark on history.

Left: Judy and Bill touring the "Big Apple", in 1966.

then take it from the grill to be eaten with my bare hands.

My first scheduled appearance was at the Cricket Club. It was estimated that nearly 25,000 attended my performance. A traveling film crew from London, England, filmed my performance, which later became a segment of the movie documentary, <u>Mondo Cane</u>. My portion of the film made me appear almost godlike. It showed people swooning, as I walked from the stage to the dressing tent. People in that part of the world had never seen anyone with my degree of physical development. I am sure any world-class bodybuilder would have had the same affect.

The trip continued to be one enlightening experience after another. We were standing at a public drinking well in one of India's major cities. The man in front of us stepped out of line, removed his loincloth, had a bowel movement and then stepped back in line. Upon reaching the well, he sat on its rim to clean himself from the well water before filling his water jug. I passed on getting a drink but watched others fill their jugs and drink, as if nothing had taken place.

On a much more pleasant note, an older man came to one of my lectures with a large box filled with rare photographs of Eugen Sandow. He had been collecting them for over fifty years. They appeared to be his most prized possession; still, he insisted that I take them as a gift. Several times I offered to pay but he refused by stating that he didn't need money. As we talked, his teeth wiggled back and forth in his mouth like blades of grass being moved by the wind.

On another occasion, I was introduced to a dignitary living in the city of Jubbulpore. He was the proud owner of a Hispano Suiza. (A car many collectors would die for.) He had purchased it new in Spain, in the early 1920s. The owner insisted that I take the car as a gift and have it shipped to California to add to my collection. I declined for several reasons, but mainly because a family of five was using the car for their home. My biggest regret returning to California was that I hadn't taken someone along to share the many unforgettable experiences.

Judy and Bill in Germany, in 1971. Talk about "Ugly Americans!"

Photograph taken by Leo Stern of Bill as they toured Rome, Italy, in 1967.

Bill tours the Far East with business associate, Tony Cardoza.

Advertising for the 1965 Reg Park Show held in Port Elizabeth, South Africa.

Chapter XXVI

AN UNEXPECTED INVITATION

Try Smiling

When the weather suits you not,
Try smiling.
When your coffee isn't hot,
Try smiling.
When your neighbors don't do right,
Or your relatives all fight,
Sure 'tis hard, but then you might
Try smiling.

Doesn't change the things, of course---
Just smiling.
But it can't make them worse---
Just smiling.
And it seems to help your case,
Brightens up a gloomy place,
Then, it sort o' rests your face---
Just smiling.

Author Unknown

I won the NABBA Professional Mr. Universe in 1967, again, by taking every first place vote. It was written, in major bodybuilding magazines, that I had secrets I wasn't sharing with the rest of the physique world. Oscar Heidenstam, editor of the British publication, *Health & Strength*, helped fuel the flames with his comments: "Let us be honest, focus was on the amazing Bill Pearl. Who, if anyone, could in any way match up to Bill? Surely the news that someone like Pearl is competing must inevitably deter those who come from a long way at considerable cost. Class 1... All the way it was Pearl, here we saw the supreme physique, posing, personality, the man himself, everything a champion should be. No superlative could describe this man. He was perfection itself, the master. It was easy for him, yet so inspiring. Who could be second to such a man? The NABBA Overall Professional Mr. Universe for 1967 just had to be Bill Pearl...and was there ever a better one?"

I had agreed to perform some feats of strength, rather than repeat a posing routine, if I was declared the overall winner of the 1967 professional contest. Leo, as usual, was there to assist.

Paul Wynter, 1966 NABBA Professional Mr. Universe, congratulates Bill on winning the 1967 Professional Mr. Universe title.

Left: Many people felt Bill was the optimum in human development.

Pearl, 1967 NABBA Professional Mr. Universe at age 37, standing next to Schwarzenegger, 1967 NABBA Amateur Mr. Universe at age 21. Both men received 100% of the judges votes.

He began priming the audience, as I changed into a black tank top, black gymnastic trousers and black sandals. I strolled back on stage carrying a duffel bag filled with auto license plates, horseshoes, 70-penny tent spikes, hot water bottles and lengths of chain.

Thanking the audience for their tremendous reception, I dug into the bag for a pair of matching California auto license plates, which I displayed before I placed the plates together, making sure that the letters were aligned. I bent the top of the plates to cause a slight crimp before speaking into the microphone, "If everything goes according to plan, I'm going to tear these two automobile plates into four pieces." Placing my right hand above the crimp, my left hand below, using my chest for support, with a pushing and twisting movement the plates tore in half. Showing them to the audience I casually mentioned, "You are going to have to be very careful when you do this, because there is a good chance you'll cut your hands on the sharp edges."

Next came a horseshoe. I tapped it against the microphone hoping for additional impact, and then gripped the shoe by both ends. With a loud grunt and a giant push/pull motion, it bent into the shape of an S. Wanting to make sure the audience was aware of what had happened, I pulled another from the bag to bend more slowly, still using the grunts for affect.

Bending the 70-penny tent spike was my toughest feat. With real effort, I bent it double, before tossing it into the audience saying, "I'll give a $1,000.00 dollars to anyone who can straighten the spike." J. Paul Getty (the world's richest man at that time) was seated in the front row. The spike accidentally landed in his lap. He apparently assumed this had been planned. Not true! Though I knew he was a fan of bodybuilding, I wasn't aware he was in the audience.

Leo and I then made a big deal out of bursting a water bottle. Showing it to the audience, I dried my lips with the back of my hand hoping for an airtight seal. Leo stood behind me to place his hands over my eyes for protection from when, or if, the bottle exploded. He began screaming out the number of my deep breaths into the water bottle. By number thirty-seven, the water bottle had grown to four feet in diameter. When the loud explosion occurred, small pieces of red rubber flew in every direction. You could almost feel the crowd's relief that it was over. I tossed the remains into the audience, bowed to the cheering crowd, as Leo and I exited the stage trying to look like it was all in a day's work. As the theater emptied, an older man jumped from his seat bellowing, "Bill Pearl is King! Bill Pearl is King!"

A gentleman in a chauffeur's uniform was waiting as we exited the rear of the theater. "At your convenience and on behalf of Mr. J. Paul Getty, I would like to invite your party to be his guests at his home, in Surrey, England, anytime in the near future." I thought someone was playing a joke. I couldn't believe J. Paul Getty, the world's richest man, was inviting us to be houseguests! I was awestruck to think that he knew we existed. Being my normal smart-ass, I said, "Please tell Mr. Getty that we're extremely busy." Arbitrarily I said something like, "It'll have to be this coming Tuesday around 10:30 a.m."

Craig Whitehead, M.D., Leo Stern and I rode in a pristine 20-year-old Cadillac Limousine to what became one of the highlights of my world travels. We exited off the main road near Surrey, England, drove a few miles, crossed bridges, went through gates, continued on past what seemed like hundreds of acres of manicured lawn adorned with centuries-old oak trees, before getting our first glimpse of Getty's 16th century, three-story castle, with its seventy-four rooms, which had once belonged to the Royal Family of England.

Mr. Getty proved to be a most gracious and humble

Tearing automobile license plates was a good way to cut your hands on the sharp edges.

Leo Stern, Craig Whitehead, M.D., J. Paul Getty and Bill take a rest while touring Mr. Getty's home in Surrey, England, which rivaled any art museum in the world.

Every room and hall of the Getty estate was furnished with priceless art work from the 16th and 17th centuries.

host. This only added to my embarrassment at being so flippant about his invitation. In spite of the fact that he worked fifteen hours a day controlling his hundred-plus corporations, he took obvious pleasure in sharing his collection of treasures. Mr. Getty personally conducted us around the estate and through the castle, and then spent hours asking and answering questions.

His collection of antiquity rivaled any art museum in the world, yet he enjoyed these priceless artifacts as everyday furnishings. We walked through rooms and halls that were hung with tapestries from 16th and 17th century Europe. The carpets and furniture had been created for Louis XIV, XV and XVI, Marie Antoinette and others. The unfortunate Anne Boleyn (second wife of England's Henry VIII, who spent her last days in the Tower of London before being beheaded) had occupied one of the massive bedrooms. The bedchamber was hung with linens used during her stay.

The tour continued to be even more breathtaking. Artifacts and sculptures of Greek and Roman antiquity lined the entrances on all three floors, accompanied by vases and urns of massive proportion. Covering most of the walls were some of the greatest works of the old masters, including: Gainsborough, Rubens, Rembrandt, Rafael, Tintoretto and even more representing Dutch, Flemish, Italian, Spanish and English artists of the 16th, 17th and 18th centuries.

It was interesting to note the lonely aspect of Getty's dining table, which was at least thirty-feet long, set with one place setting and a bottle of A-1 Steak Sauce. We were equally impressed with the estate's security. The grounds were crisscrossed with wire dog runs, patrolled by dozens of Dobermans. At night, more Dobermans paced the halls of the castle until dawn.

Mr. Getty remained a thoughtful host to the end of our visit. After we signed his guest book, he showed us to the front steps and stood waving goodbye, until we saw him become a small figure in the distance.

Bill and Mr. Getty posing outside the Getty estate. Mr. Getty remained a thoughtful host to the end of their visit.

133

Chapter XXVII

HOORAY FOR HOLLYWOOD

All The World's a Stage
(As You Like It.)
All the world's a stage,
And all the men and women merely players:
They have their exits and their entrances;
And one man in his time plays many parts.

William Shakespeare

There is a slight possibility I could have had an acting career if I'd pursued it with half the intensity that went into my weight training. In the mid-1960s, several movie roles became available. In the movie Muscle Beach Party starring Annette Funacello, they were simulating a bodybuilding competition. The director didn't have a clue about physiques. He only cared that the most photogenic bodybuilder appeared as the winner, which wasn't me. I told him, "I've beaten most of these guys in real competition. If I'm not the winner, I'm out of here!" He didn't argue, as I was marched off the set.

In Jupiter's Daughter starring Esther Williams, a specific scene was going to skyrocket me to stardom. Ms. Williams was supposedly exploring an ancient city that had been submerged underwater for thousands of years. I was one of a dozen bodybuilders hired to act as live underwater statues, while she swam over, around and under us. The scene was shot outdoors in a huge water tank during the coldest time in southern California's history. The extras were obliged to be on the set from 9:00 a.m. until 5:00 p.m. Ms. Williams had a beautiful portable heated dressing room to lounge in, while we stood around in wet bathing suits. A few days into the shooting, I decided that dying from hypothermia wasn't worth the fame and fortune. I again walked off the set.

Working in television wasn't much better. Problems on the Regis Philbin Show began the moment his co-host complained how disappointed she was that I hadn't lugged a 150-pound barbell all over Hollywood, so Regis could impress their audience by lifting it. Everything went downhill from there. The first question out of Mr. Philbin's mouth was, "Bill, why do so many homosexuals

weight train?" My response was, "Regis, I can't speak from firsthand knowledge, but probably because it is one of the best ways to stay physically fit."

Better success came from working on the weekly television show, The Hollywood Palace. When the casting director wanted someone who looked athletic, or was needed to cushion the fall of a guest celebrity, I got the call. I worked with Steve Allen, Groucho Marks, Edie Adams, Ed Wynn, Ernie Kovacks, Betty Davis, Gloria Swanson, Sammy Davis, Jr. and Juliette Prowse, the terrific dancer from South Africa. She couldn't resist asking, "What are you? A holdover from Kismet?" (Kismet was a New York stage play that had featured several bodybuilders and had closed several years earlier.)

One of the perks that came with working on The Hollywood Palace was the time spent at Western Costumes being outfitted. On a segment featuring Forest Tucker of F-Troop, an American Indian was needed for a stand-in. While being fitted in full Native American regalia, I noticed an old opera hat sitting on a shelf, with an arrow stuck through it. The hat had been used in the movie, Northwest Passage, starring Spencer Tracy. I loved the movie. I loved the hat and loved it even more as it sat waiting to be tried on. To my great pleasure, it fit my giant head perfectly. I stood admiring myself in a mirror thinking, "Hat, where were you when I was a ten-year old kid?"

My most successful film venture came with the starring role in the movie Voodoo Swamp, produced and directed by Arthur Jones, who later became famous as the owner and inventor of Nautilus exercise equipment. The

Left: For Bill, Hollywood, California, was a far cry from Yakima, Washington.

movie was filmed in Louisiana and Florida, but nearly died on a cutting room floor in California. Arthur still insists that it had the potential of becoming a "cult classic."

Arthur personally came to Sacramento, California, to offer me the part in <u>Voodoo Swamp</u>. Whether I possessed any acting ability had little bearing on his decision to hire me. He was looking for the world's most muscular white man, and I apparently filled the bill.

My role was to play the part of a good guy/bodybuilder who had gone to New Orleans, Louisiana. I somehow had gotten lost in the Everglades only to be found by a lady witch doctor who had the ability to put me under her spell. This changed me into a monster that allowed me to do horrific things, on her behalf. Fortunately, I was recaptured before the filming ended and brought back to civilization, to return to the good guy/bodybuilder.

When filming began, my wardrobe consisted of underwear, socks, a shirt, trousers and shoes. Over the next four weeks, my clothing was ripped bit by bit with the idea of making me look more ragged while showing more muscle. Towards the end of shooting, I was down to

wearing a half torn T-shirt with pants that looked like cutoffs. Thankfully, filming ended on time. My only item of clothing left in reserve was a pair of boxer shorts.

Bert Goodrich (in suit), Joe Gold (number 12), Steve Reeves (number 13) and Zabo Kozewski (kneeling). All were movie stars.

The role Pearl played in <u>Voodoo Swamp</u> was the part of a good guy/bodybuilder, who was under the spell of the lady witch doctor.

Chapter XXVIII

AN UNCONVENTIONAL CHARACTER

Should You Feel Inclined to Censure

Should you feel inclined to censure
Faults you may in others view,
Ask your own heart, ere you venture,
If you have not failings, too.
Let not friendly vows be broken;
Rather strive a friend to gain.
Many words in anger spoken
Find their passage home again.

Do not, then, in idle pleasure
Trifle with a brother's fame;
Guard it as a valued treasure,
Sacred as your own good name.

Do not form opinions blindly;
Hastiness to trouble tends;
Those of whom we thought unkindly
Oft become our warmest friends.

Author Unknown

It's impossible to overlook this opportunity to give you more insight on the Arthur Jones I know. He is, by far, one of the most unique individuals I've ever met. Mike Mentzer (former IFBB Mr. America winner) attempted to describe Arthur by stating, "Arthur Jones is not a relaxing person to be with. He does not lightly exchange words. He spews facts, torrents of them, gleaned from studies and perhaps more important, from practical application of theory, personal observations and incisive deduction. You don't converse with Arthur Jones: you attend his lectures. He is opinionated, challenging, intense and blunt."

I am in total agreement with Mike. This is just a taste of our on-again/off-again relationship, which began in 1958. Early one Monday morning, while I was opening the door to my Sacramento gym, Arthur appeared out of nowhere. He was wearing khaki pants, a khaki shirt and jacket that half-covered a .357 Magnum pistol strapped to his belt.

In his heavily southern accented, no-nonsense, baritone voice, he began the introduction, "You're Bill Pearl. My name is Arthur Jones. I'm from Slidell, Louisiana. I've come to see if you're interested in participating in a 'gawd'-damn movie I'm going to produce. I'll need you for about a month. It's going to be filmed in Florida and Louisiana."

I asked, "Do you make movies for a living?" He articulated every word with a slight pause in between to make sure that he wouldn't have to repeat himself, "Hell, no. I have a large wildlife game reserve in Slidell that

Left: Arthur Jones' decision to build his $75 million corporate headquarters in Lake Helen, Florida, put the small town on the map. He claimed his privately held company had a reported estimated annual income of $300 million and was the world's largest manufacturer of exercise machines.

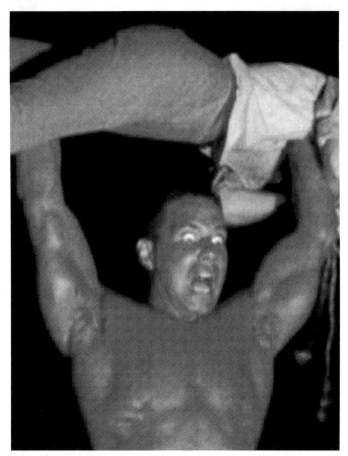

"Look out below!," Bill in the movie Voodoo Swamp produced by Arthur Jones, in 1958.

supplies most of the animal parks and zoos throughout the country with reptiles, exotic birds, monkeys and other 'gawd'-damn wildlife that I capture in South America. But I'm not new to the film business. I've made several documentaries." "When do you plan to start filming?" I asked. "As soon as I can get your ass down to Louisiana." "What am I supposed to do in this movie?" "Whatever it takes to make the 'gawd'-damn thing sell!" "How much are you willing to pay?" "How much are you worth?" We agreed on a price and, to this day, I've never picked up a tab when we've been together. His pride seemed offended whenever I've tried.

During those few days in Sacramento, it became obvious that we were from different worlds. Arthur had a definite opinion on everything. When it came to bodybuilding, he was convinced that the fastest muscular gains came from doing, "One set per muscle group--three days per week--while training to failure."

On politics, I asked, "Do you think John F. Kennedy will become the next President of the United States?" His reply, "It really doesn't matter. Some right-thinking Texan will take care of the son-of-a-bitch."

Our differences became more obvious during the

filming of his movie Voodoo Swamp. Arthur could survive on Coca-Cola and cigarettes while holding court with whomever until the wee hours of the morning, and then expect everyone to be ready to go at his beck and call. I needed food, rest and consistency.

We clashed about a week into the filming. Six of us were jammed in his new Oldsmobile station wagon traveling to shoot a scene that had me trudging up to my neck in swamp water filled with leeches. The car radio was tuned to a country station blaring so loud it was impossible to think. He made matters worse by chain smoking in the closed vehicle. I was dragging from lack of sleep, and a white bread bologna sandwich wasn't my idea of a balanced diet.

Things came to a head when he began playing 'grab-ass' with the script girl sitting between us. I sat thinking, "This is ridiculous." I flicked off the radio and shouted, "Stop the car!" Arthur retaliated with, "Why? You got a 'gawd'-damn problem?" I shouted, "I've got several problems! First, I can't breathe! Second, I don't do well on bologna sandwiches! Third, I've had as much sleep this past week, as I normally get in a night. Now you two decide to start screwing around. Either there are some drastic changes, or I'm out of here!" He apologized by saying something like, "I didn't realize you were so 'gawd'-damn sensitive."

The more violent side of Arthur erupted while we were shooting a night scene that had me throwing a stunt man off a bridge into a large pool of water. We had done the scene several times, which always ended in a big splash, but on the final take, there was a thud. The stunt man had landed on the bank rather than in the water. With a loud moan he cried, "Arthur--if we're going to do this again, make sure Mr. Pearl tosses me further to the left!"

A carload of teenage boys had stopped to watch the filming. As they drove away, a crew member called out that he was missing an expensive camera. He was insistent that the teenagers had taken it.

In less than a block, they were pulled over. Arthur ran to their car screaming, "Did one of you steal my 'gawd'-damn camera?" There was no response. Arthur pulled out his pistol, drew back the hammer, placed the barrel in the middle of the driver's forehead saying, "Boy, I'm going to ask you one more time, before I scatter your 'gawd'-damn brains all over this car! Did one of you steal my 'gawd'-damn camera?" His reputation must have preceded him. The driver stuttered, "Honest Mr. Jones, we did not ta--ta-

-take your camera." Not satisfied, Arthur told me to begin searching the car. Fortunately, one of his crew ran up screaming that they had found it stored in the back of the station wagon. It seemed everyone but Arthur let out a sigh, as he eased back the hammer of the gun.

In our final days of filming, Arthur had rented a beautiful old mansion on the outskirts of New Orleans. I was to be kept imprisoned in the mansion while recovering from the lady witch doctor's spell. They had me tied to beds, chairs, or whatever, to prevent me from causing more harm. Arthur had left instructions for Shorty, the head cameraman, to shoot a scene in the enormous living room where I was tied between two large pillars.

Shorty, like Arthur, was a chain smoker. He had a bad habit of setting lighted cigarettes on everything, which began to take its toll on the beautiful antique furnishings. What upset me even more was that he'd drop the butts on the marble floors, and then grind them out with the soles of his shoes. I finally told him, "Shorty, you do that one more time, and I'm going to bounce you on your can." Sure enough, the next cigarette out of his mouth went on the floor to be ground to death. I jerked out of the ties and hit him so hard it knocked him, the camera, the tripod, the lights and canisters of film onto the floor.

Arthur heard the commotion and ran into the room shouting, "What-n-the-'gawd'-damn- hell's going on here?" Shorty looked up, saying, "He just hit me, and I bet he broke the camera." Arthur asked, "Why in the hell did you do that?" I replied, "Because he has destroyed half of the antique furniture in this house with his lousy cigarettes and is now doing the same to the marble floors. It's going to cost you more money for repairs, than you'll make from the movie." Arthur looked at Shorty and said something like, "You stupid moron. I should blow your 'gawd'-damn brains out." I returned to Sacramento without ever seeing the finished version of the movie.

Several months later, Arthur invited me to view his latest film that he shot and produced in Africa. The screening took place in a private Hollywood studio. I had no idea what to expect, but knew it would not be a sequel to the movie Lassie. The least violent part of the two-hour documentary was the opening scene. It showed several natives dragging an enormous crocodile from a lake. The natives were close to losing limbs, as they struggled to get the crocodile subdued and turned over on its back, before Arthur stepped in with a huge knife to slit open its belly to pull out a young boy.

After another lapse of time, Arthur phoned from the Los Angeles International Airport asking if he could stay with me for a few days. I had moved from Sacramento to Los Angeles and was living close to the airport in the apartment above the Manchester Gym with a spare bedroom--so--"Sure!"

He was back to supplying animal parks and zoos with reptiles, exotic birds, monkeys and other 'gawd'-damn wildlife. He was headed for the Galapagos Islands, located six hundred fifty miles west of Ecuador.

After keeping me up most of the night, he went to a corner cafe the following morning for coffee. I walked into the spare bedroom to find several large stacks of one hundred dollar bills lying on the bed, which had not been slept in. The apartment had been broken into a couple of weeks before, which caused me more than a little anxiety seeing somewhere between $35,000.00 and $50,000.00 in cash lying out in plain view. When Arthur returned, I suggested that he find a better place for his money. Later, I asked, "Why are you carrying so much cash?" His answer, "Money talks, especially American money."

Weeks went by before another phone call from Arthur, which originated from the Los Angeles International Airport's freight depot. Offering no explanation, Arthur barked, "Bill, this is a matter of life and death! I want you to immediately go to the produce mart in Los Angeles. Pick up five-hundred pounds of 'gawd'-damn bananas! Bring them to the United Air Lines freight depot as quickly as possible." (The telephone went click.)

I was at the produce mart in twenty minutes. I found an outdoor fruit stand and didn't bother shopping prices or explaining why I was buying five-hundred pounds of "'gawd'-damned bananas;" I didn't know myself.

The United Air Lines freight depot's loading dock was filled with crates of exotic birds. Arthur was running around screaming, "The 'gawd'-damn things are going to die if they don't get food and water. You continue filling the water dishes, I'll do the rest."

He eventually calmed down, but insisted he had to travel in the cargo hold of the airplane to be sure the birds were fed and watered on their trip to Slidell. He was told to go the United Air Lines main terminal to obtain permission.

Standing next in line at the ticket counter, I watched Arthur get a pained look on his face while, through clenched teeth he screamed, "My 'gawd'-damn hemorrhoids are killing me." The female ticket agent and everyone close by gasped as he loosened his pants and jammed his right hand down the back of his shorts to take care of the problem. Squaring himself away before stepping up to the counter, he offered the agent his tickets with the hand that had just performed the miracle. She bellowed out, "I can't take this! I'm calling my supervisor!" He looked at me, saying, "What the 'gawd'-damn hell's wrong with her?"

When we first met in Sacramento, one of our original discussions had been on strength training. Arthur had shown particular interest in a new Selectorized arm-curl machine that had been designed by my friend Bob Clark. The machine used an off-centered cam that caused the resistance to vary as the user curled the lever arm through its range of motion.

There was no need to explain Clark's concept of using the off-centered cam to alter the resistance of an exercise to Arthur. He was well aware of the benefits. In fact, he went on a tirade that not only covered strength curves, but also the amount of energy stored in muscles, the recovery time between workouts, and the benefits of shorter, all-out effort training sessions. He was so convincing, my hard-core bodybuilders couldn't wait to

Arm curl machine with an off-centered cam, designed by Bob Clark, in the year 1958.

give his system of training a try. Twelve years later, when he launched his new line of Nautilus exercise machines, he was still using the same pitch.

Arthur founded Nautilus Sports/Medical Industries, in 1970. His new line of exercise machines became so popular over the next ten years, it was said that more money was spent on Nautilus than on all other commercial gym equipment being sold.

The first version of his machine was previewed in Culver City, California, at that year's AAU Mr. America Contest. I acted as Master of Ceremonies. My training partner, Chris Dickerson, became the first Afro-American to win the title.

Arthur had transported the prototype from Slidell, to Culver City, in a rented trailer. To save money, he stayed at our home in Pasadena. His 13-year-old son, Gary, remarked with confidence, "We can put another inch on your arm in a month, if you will use the machine."

The Nautilus multi-station unit that sat in the lobby of the Culver City convention hall looked like a bad substitute for the popular Universal multi-station unit. Arthur's unit was cumbersome, poorly built, painted blue and equipped with lever arms to hold free-weights. It was immediately nicknamed "The Blue Monster." Its best selling points were Arthur's gift-of-gab and the off-centered cams, which were pitched to everyone who would listen.

I later commented to Arthur that trying to compete against the Universal multi-station unit might be a mistake. I suggested that he design separate pieces of equipment incorporating the off-centered cam and then promote his theory of training, which could only be done "on his machines." How much influence my suggestion had on his decision to do this is anyone's guess, but that's what eventually evolved.

At the beginning of the Nautilus reign, Arthur used the editorial pages of *Iron Man* magazine to promote his concepts. Issue after issue was filled with his opinions on training. The magazine was so hard-core, its readers were more than willing to give Arthur's theories a try, if they could get their hands on his equipment. Sales of his units were going out of sight. Prospective buyers were phoning my gym day and night to confirm what Arthur was preaching. There were so many calls, in fact, that it started interfering with my ability to run my business. He convinced me that my time wasn't being wasted. In exchange, he was going to give me the new Nautilus Biceps/Triceps and Torso Pullover machines, *plus* an exclusive written Nautilus franchise for the State of California.

He then tried to convince me that bodybuilding had changed since my last competition in 1967. The only way I could win the 1971 NABBA Professional contest was by following his training principles, along with incorporating the Nautilus machines into my programs. It mattered little that I'd done quite well with free weights for twenty-five years. When the Biceps/Triceps and Torso Pullover machines arrived, I placed them in the living room of our home for my own personal use. Later, to Judy's relief, they were transferred to the gym, where they became so popular it was nearly impossible to get near them.

Our relationship became more strained when I informed Arthur that I had replaced the lever arms of my Nautilus machines in the Pasadena Health Club with weight stacks. Arthur went ballistic saying, "You ruined the 'gawd'-damn biomechanics by doing that." My reply was, "Arthur, you're wrong. The movement is even better. Because of the weight stacks you now start the motion from a dead stop rather than having a swinging motion. Besides, there are no weight plates to pick up, the machines are more simple, safer and faster to use." "Yah... but... but," he sputtered. Later it occurred to me that Arthur might not have been so upset because I ruined the 'gawd'-damn biomechanics of his machines, as he was with the fact that he was now going to have to add weight stacks to the machines he was currently manufacturing. It was possible that he didn't have the capital to make the conversion at that time.

It came down to where I either had to replace the lever arms on my machines, or he was going to renege on the exclusive Nautilus franchise for California. Stupidly, I told him it would be a relief to get back to running my gym. That remark probably cost me millions of dollars from the profits of the sales of Nautilus in the State of California, over the next several years.

Matters didn't improve when I publicly questioned Arthur's theories regarding the advantages that came from training on the Nautilus Isokinetic machines. Much of the promotional material in the early days of Nautilus was based on the claim that free weights were obsolete, injury-causing antiques. I disagreed. He claimed that three twenty-minute workouts per week on Nautilus equipment could produce a physique like mine. Again, I

The relationship between Arthur and Bill became more strained when Bill replaced the lever arms of the Nautilus Biceps/Triceps machine with weight stacks.

disagreed by stating, "Nobody who has trained exclusively on Nautilus has won a major physique contest." This enraged Arthur to the extent that he began threatening Leo and me with phone taps and hit men. Why he included Leo is anyone's guess.

He used *Iron Man* magazine to wage his war, which became more venomous with each issue. The final straw occurred when he commented that it was "rumored" that my training partner, twenty-eight-year-old Willie Stedman, had died because of anabolic steroid use, which I supposedly had supplied. It was sadly true that Willy had died, but the cause of death was pneumonia, brought on by a lethal strain of Asian flu. I contacted Peary Rader, the owner and publisher of *Iron Man* magazine, threatening a lawsuit if a retraction wasn't printed.

I kept training for the 1971 NABBA Mr. Universe, using the same methods that had brought the best results in the past. By now, Arthur was so irate it was "rumored" that he had given Sergio Oliva $5,000.00 to come to

Florida to train on Nautilus with a promise of another $5,000.00, if he won the contest.

To rattle me even more, Arthur sent recent photos of Sergio with a note reading something like, "What do you think about this?" I sent the photos back with a note, saying, "I have never seen YOU looking better. There is a good chance, if YOU can stay in that kind of condition, YOU might place high in the contest."

Before leaving for London, I gave my final warm-up exhibition in Brooklyn, New York. The backstage was loaded with bodybuilding celebrities: Boyer Coe, Mike and Ray Mentzer, Dave Draper to mention a few. Again, Arthur appeared out of nowhere. He began showing everyone recent photos of Sergio, asking for comment. When he noticed I was ignoring him, he turned, handed me the photos, saying in a loud voice, "What do you think?" I replied, "He looks great--you look like shit." Turning a couple of shades of red, possibly more out of embarrassment than anger, he began muttering

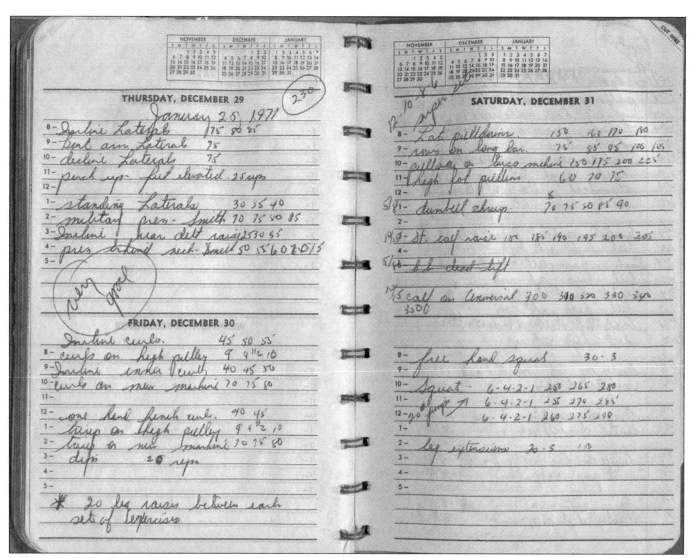

The training program Bill used just prior to the 1971 NABBA Professional Mr. Universe contest.

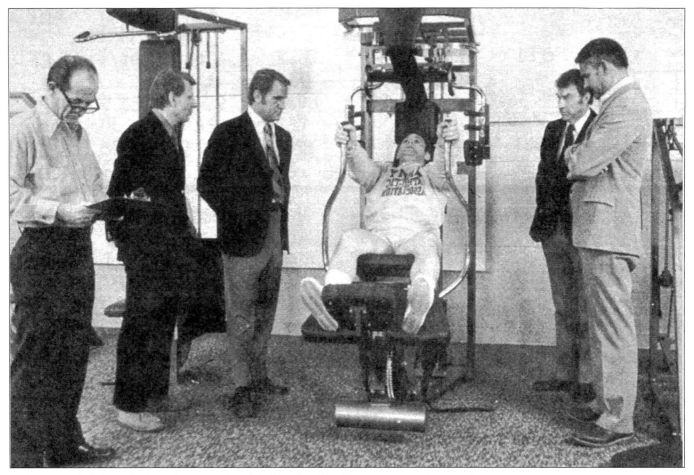

Arthur Jones, far left, conducting a demonstration of the Nautilus Chest Press to a group of prospective customers.

something about getting his gun. Before he finished the sentence, I said, "If you come back with a gun, I'm going to stick it up your butt and blow your brains out!"

On Friday, September 18, 1971, the Victoria Palace in London, England, was packed for the 23rd annual NABBA Mr. Universe contest. Leo, his wife, and Judy were seated near the front row, Arthur several rows behind. The audience anxiously waited until the last announcements were made. "Ladies and gentlemen, the 1971 NABBA Amateur Mr. Universe for 1971 is--Ken Waller of the United States." The Master of Ceremonies, Cecil Peck, went on, "The 1971 NABBA Professional Mr. Universe is (he stopped for a long pause) Bill Pearl!" The crowd went wild. After I received the trophy, Reg Park walked over to congratulate me while Sergio Oliva and Frank Zane walked offstage.

A few years elapsed with no word from Arthur; then again a knock on our door. Arthur, his wife, and their business partner, Dan Baldwin, were standing on the porch. I remarked, "If you're man enough to come to our home, the least I can do is invite you in." Once seated, it became obvious that everyone was on his best behavior-- except Judy. The following is her version of that day:

"One peaceful Sunday morning, there was a knock on our door. I opened to find Arthur, his wife, and Dan Baldwin, standing on our porch. I closed the door in their faces before leaving to tell Bill. He shook Arthur's hand, as if nothing had happened. The next is his recollection as to my obstinate refusal of hospitality. When Bill offered them coffee, my reply was, "We don't have coffee in the house. We're not drinking caffeinated products." He then offered them tea. My response was, "We only have herbal tea." He then asked if they would like milk or sugar. I informed him, " We don't have any milk or refined sugar, only brown raw sugar." The response was, "That'll be fine."

Once Judy sat with our guests, she couldn't help but admire Arthur's intellect and vision. He began describing a system for health clubs that would incorporate a membership card that could be swiped into the terminal of several exercise machines, which received their resistance from a computer controlled electronic motor. The machines would record the member's workout and at the end of the training session, print a read-out, or store the material for future reference. Arthur was describing in the early 1970s what became in the 1990s the Lifecircuit®

and Lifecenter®, produced by Life Fitness. The visit ended peacefully with never a mention of any break in our relationship or why he had suddenly decided to "drop by."

We stayed in touch, but with long gaps in between. I appeared on two of his weekly <u>Wild Cargo</u> television shows. My job was to take gunnysacks filled with venomous cobra snakes and dump them on the floor of the television studio as the cameras recorded Arthur's ability to toy with deadly reptiles. On another occasion he flew me from Las Vegas, Nevada, to Los Angeles, California, in his private jet. Months later, I attended a lecture at the University of Virginia where he was extremely hard on the medical profession, telling the audience what a 'gawd'-damn bunch of misfits they were. Later, I toured the Nautilus factory in Deland, Florida, which was indeed impressive.

With time, we grew even further apart. When I phoned, his usual reaction was, "What the 'gawd'-damn hell do you want?" His latest comeback when asked how he was doing, was, "I'm sitting here waiting to die."

Our last face-to-face visit occurred in 2001 at his home in Ocala, Florida. At the age of seventy-nine, he claimed to be in poor health, but his mind was as sharp as ever. Sitting on a sofa, wearing only a bathrobe that revealed everything from his chest down, his first words were, "It's been 43 years, 5 months and 26 days since we first met." The next couple of hours were spent rehashing research he'd done on negative training in the 1980s. The rest of the time was taken up by his recitation of the mistakes I'd made over the years. I was able to point out a few of his. Yet, I couldn't help but thank him for the profound impact he'd had on my life. I closed the visit by saying, "Arthur, you've been a good teacher." His reply, "Well, school is over! This is the last 'gawd'-damn time we'll see each other." As I reached to shake his hand, he lit another cigarette.

Robert Mills and Bill encouraging a Lifecircuit® user during the 1995 FIBO Show in Essen, Germany.

This page has been intentionally left blank.

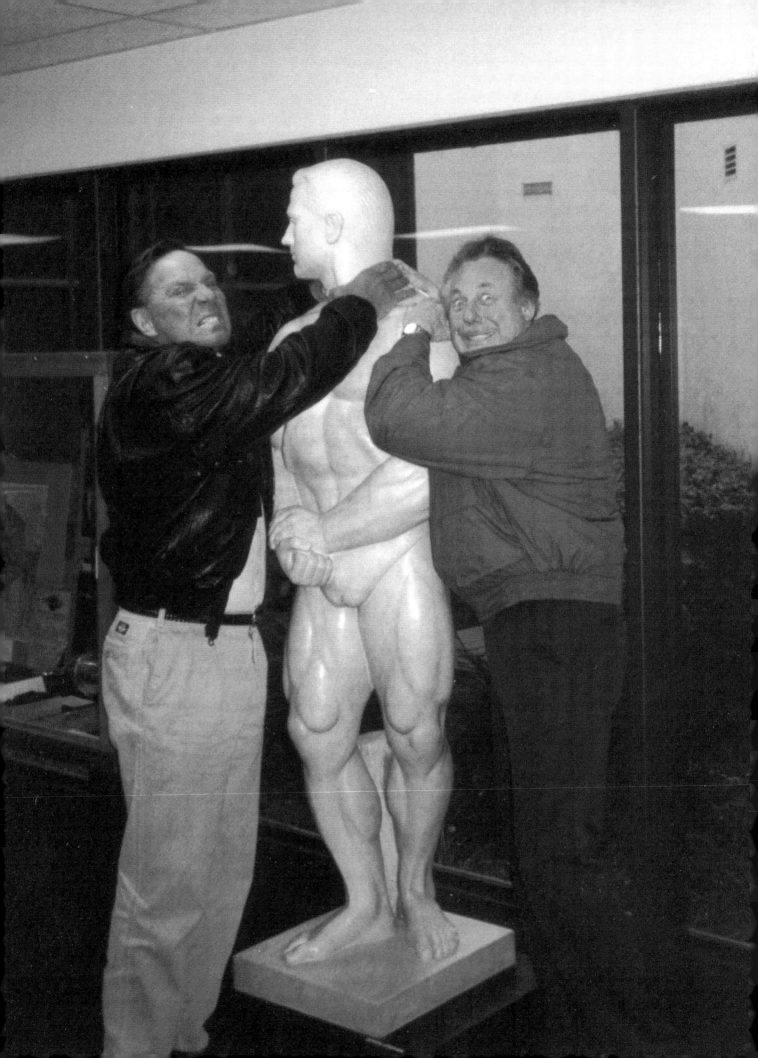

Chapter XXIX

TO EACH HIS OWN

Good Timber

The tree that never had to fight
For sun and sky and air and light,
But stood out in the open plain
And always got its share of rain,
Never became a forest king
But lived and died a scrubby thing.

The man who never had to toil
To gain and farm his patch of soil,
Who never had to win his share
Of sun and sky and light and air,
Never became a manly man
But lived and died as he began.

Good timber does not grow with ease,
The stronger wind, the stronger trees,
The further sky, the greater length,
The more the storm, the more the strength,
By sun and cold, by rain and snow,
In trees and men good timbers grow.

Where thickest lies the forest growth
We find the patriarchs of both.
And they hold counsel with the stars
Whose broken branches show the scars
Of many winds and much of strife
This is the common law of life.

Douglas Malloch

During the 1940s and 1950s, John Grimek's physique was so outstanding most everyone in the sport followed his principles of training. If John trained a specific way, it had to be right. When I saw photos of Grimek, my eyes were automatically drawn to his massive calves. Every article published that mentioned his calf training was a repeat of what had previously been written: three sets of standing calf raises, for twenty to twenty-five reps, using moderate weight, three days a week. This method for training calves became gospel. If anyone wanted calves like Grimek's, you did what John did.

What most readers, including myself, failed to realize was that John's calves would have been amazing regardless of the three sets of standing calf raises, for twenty to twenty-five reps, using moderate weight, three days a week. I never thought to question why my calves hadn't responded to his program. I should have known better. By keeping training records, it was obvious that my body responded best to several sets, less reps, heavier weights... why would my calves be different?

Left: Bill and George Coates doing a job on the marble statue of Grimek in the York Barbell Hall of Fame.

Reg Park and wife, Maréon, visit Sylvia and Bill at their home in Sacramento, California, in the mid 1950s.

Reg Park, a man's man in every sense of the word. The photograph is from the movie <u>Hercules and the Captive Women</u>.

With that in mind, I designed a training program for calves around what I knew the rest of my body responded to. I continued doing standing calf raises but increased the sets from three to fifteen... (five sets, toes facing out... five sets, feet straight... five sets, toes facing in.) I dropped the repetitions to twelve, used nearly all the weight that I could handle and still do the exercise properly. I did these five days per week rather than three days. The results? My calves jumped from 17 to 19 inches in three months. The results were so encouraging, I decided to step out of the mold of doing things simply because others had done them a certain way. I decided to become more reliant on myself to find the correct answers for the degree of physical development I was hoping for.

I met Reg Park in London, England, in 1953. He had already acquired the notoriety that I was hoping for by winning the NABBA Mr. Universe in 1951. What drew me closer to him, other than his being another of my heroes, was that we had similar thoughts on weight training. When either visited the United States, or England, we made it a point to work out with each other.

We agreed to share training ideas. I began splitting

my workouts according to body parts: Mondays, Wednesday and Fridays: abs, chest, shoulders, triceps, biceps and calves. Tuesdays, Thursdays and Saturdays: abs, back, thighs, calves, forearms and neck. The results were so impressive, I couldn't wait to pass this on to Reg.

In a return letter, he commented that he was experimenting on a different system of training: a muscle group in the morning, another in the afternoon, and another in the evening. I can't remember how he was splitting this program, but do remember that his strength was increasing by leaps and bounds. He was doing sets and reps of bench presses with over four-hundred pounds and knocking out five-hundred-pound full-squats, without the aid of a spotter or training partner.

Even though our training regimen varied, we were following a similar approach. Whereas the average bodybuilder would do regular bench presses for three sets with ten to fifteen repetitions and then stop, we went so far as to do regular bench presses, incline bench presses, and decline bench presses for five sets with six to ten repetitions.

We followed this type of regimen for each muscle

group for four to six weeks before making changes that might have included a different group of exercises, a variation in the sets or repetitions, possibly pyramiding the weight up and down, perhaps super-setting, tri-setting--anything that sounded legitimate.

At that stage of my training, more time was spent reading anatomy and physiology books than bodybuilding magazines. My conclusion was that the best exercises (if there are such things) were those that worked muscles through a complete contraction and extension, while doing the movements from different angles; standing, seated, inclined, or declined had the most positive affect.

Triceps became my most impressive muscle group because of heavy overhead movements. I chose those types of exercise by studying how the muscle attached to the skeletal structure. I again concluded that any overhead movement done by keeping the upper arms in a vertical position overhead, while lowering a weight in a concentrated semicircular motion until the forearms and biceps touched, before returning the weight to the overhead starting position, would affect the large head of the triceps more than any other movement. I then determined that it was also important to work all three heads of the muscle. I made sure this happened during each triceps training session.

Through those, and several other types of innovations, Reg and I brought in a new era to bodybuilding. We came up with workable programs that were producing more size, shape and muscularity. We weren't afraid to share with others. We did this via photographs and articles that appeared in physique magazines throughout the world.

Bodybuilders who migrated to the P-Street Gym in Sacramento, California, were using these principles. They were winning major contests on the West Coast and returning home to win State Championships. Ray Routledge (winner of the 1961 AAU Mr. America and 1961 NABBA Amateur Mr. Universe) was a slight exception. It seemed he had nothing but time on his hands. He would hit the gym around 5:00 each evening, do a set then sit for five or ten minutes. It was always the same story come 10:00 p.m. closing time, "Just a couple more sets," he'd say. Twenty minutes later, again it was, "Just a couple more sets." My alternative was to lock him in the gym with the threat of bodily harm if he exited during the night leaving the deadbolt unlocked.

Bill's upper arm measured over 20 inches at a body weight of around 220 pounds.

Ray Routledge winning the 1961 NABBA Amateur Mr. Universe title.

Chapter XXX

PRE-CONTEST STRATEGY

The Champion
The average runner sprints
Until the breath in him is gone;
But the champion has the iron will;
That makes him carry on.

For rest, the average runner begs,
When limp his muscles grow;
But the champion runs on leaden legs
His spirit makes him go.

The average man's complacent
When he does his best to score;
But the champion does his best
And then he does a little more.

Author Unknown

It is likely that I could have won the NABBA Mr. Universe title several years in a row but that wasn't my objective. Every four or five years, a new crop of bodybuilders would emerge, which caused my curiosity and ego to step in. I'd give myself a year in advance to prepare for the competition. During that time, everything revolved around the upcoming contest. Not capable of handling heavier weights or training with more intensity, attitude and eating habits were the main items to focus on.

Rather than gaining several pounds of body weight months prior a competition, and then cutting down, I would purposely drop body weight to where my body fat registered somewhere between three to five percent, before deciding on the body weight and percentage of lean muscle mass I wanted to carry for the contest. My decision was always a heavier body weight with more lean muscle than my previous competitions. Our family diet had changed to lacto-ovo-vegetarian by the mid-1960s, which made this more difficult to do. Red meat, fish or fowl were no longer part of our eating habits. (Our family is still lacto-ovo-vegetarian.)

My pre-contest weight loss regimen consisted of three

small meals per day, totaling between 2000-2500 calories. Protein and some fat were the main sources of these calories, along with moderate quantities of fresh fruits and vegetables. A typical breakfast might be three poached eggs, low fat cottage cheese, and fruit; lunch was homemade soups, full of lentils, beans, cabbage, carrots, tomatoes, celery and onions; and supper most likely would be an omelet, a big salad and a diet soft drink. Treats would be extra fruit, high in fiber but low in calories.

I did not go from eating like a bird to feasting like a monster. It was more of a gradual increase of food and with time, protein and complex carbohydrates became even more important. I would begin adding milk and egg-white based caseinate protein drinks and larger quantities of assorted fresh vegetables and fruit throughout the day to gradually increase my caloric intake. Getting close to contest time, I'd consume around fourteen ounces of milk and egg protein powder per day.

Posing, eliminating body hair and getting sun were just part of the attitude change. Here, self-hypnosis came into play. After each meal and training session, I'd relax for a few minutes, programming myself to become bigger,

Left: At this stage of Pearl's bodybuilding career, he had changed to a lacto-ovo-vegetarian diet and was still able to maintain his massive size.

MUSCULAR DEVELOPMENT

50c
PDC

FEBRUARY 1964

HOW YOU CAN GET BIGGER and BETTER ARMS!

HOW I GAINED 50 POUNDS OF SOLID MUSCLE by coverman BILL PEARL

Developing a SHAPELY and MUSCULAR Torso

WHEN IS "ENOUGH" EXERCISE?

How you can IMPROVE Your Posing

MUSCULAR DEVELOPMENT

DEVOTED TO THE SCIENCE OF BODYBUILDING

It is likely that Bill could have won the NABBA Mr Universe title several years in a row, if that had been his interest. He competed in a total of eleven contests during his nearly twenty-year bodybuilding career.

154

Billy Knight, Mr. Australia, and Brad Krayer were two of Bill's best training partners.

Terry Edwards, Rocco Castalino, Mike Tonkinson (seated) and Kevin Robbins were also great believers in early morning training.

Bill curling a 135-pound barbell.

One of the more powerful bodybuilders, Bill was credited with a seated-press-behind-neck of 300 pounds and curling 100-pound dumbbells.

stronger and more muscular. At night I'd lull myself to sleep saying, "When I awake I will be bigger, stronger, and more muscular." All thoughts revolved around getting bigger, stronger and more muscular. I never thought, smaller, weaker, or less muscular. Nothing could be small! Small wouldn't get it. Big was going to get it.

There was no time for negativism. Training began at 4:00 a.m. Monday through Saturday. Partners were chosen that could be counted on to spot for each other, help change weights and encourage one another to train harder. It was a win/win situation. Much of my success came from never resting on laurels. Leo and I always thought I could do better. We were never satisfied.

Chapter XXXI

WIN SOME...LOSE SOME

Hold Fast Your Dreams

Hold fast your dreams!
Within your heart
Keep one still, secret spot
Where dreams may go,
And, sheltered so,
May thrive and grow
Where doubt and fear are not.
O keep a place apart,
Within your heart,
For little dreams to go!

Louise Driscoll

My four-year military enlistment had ended. My plan was to get into the gym business. Don Farnsworth, my ex-Navy friend, kept hounding me to come to Sacramento. The city had a population of 200,000 with one poorly operated health club and a YMCA that was no better. We spent several days looking for real estate agents or landlords who would take a twenty-three year old with a $2,800.00 bank account seriously.

Finally, we found a suitable location close to downtown Sacramento on 19th and P Streets. The building took one front window space plus the back of three other businesses to make up the 4,000-square foot, L shaped, non-air conditioned area. I signed a five-year lease, thanked Don for sharing his apartment, bought an army cot, then moved in.

The gym became my home for the next several months. During that interval, Sylvia Frazier and I were married. Following a two-day honeymoon in Las Vegas, Nevada, she returned to San Diego, California, to live with her family, until I was able to afford an apartment in Sacramento.

The previous tenant of the gym area seemed to have forgotten an enormous printing press that straddled a 5-foot wide, 20-foot long, and 4-foot deep cement pit lodged in the middle of the to-be exercise area. As my rent-free status was about to end and my phone complaints went unanswered, I reverted to my religious upbringing of "an

eye for an eye." I began removing the most intricate parts off the printing press to toss them into the bottom of the pit, which was half filled with printers ink. When the press was finally moved, we immediately filled the pit with sand and concrete.

Bill Pearl's Gym was a crude affair. The majority of the equipment had been built at the Naval Recreation Center in San Diego. The locker room consisted of two benches and a Sears Roebuck metal shower. A friend painted "BILL PEARL'S GYM" in twenty-four-inch letters on the front window. My only affordable advertising was word of mouth. Most of the small profit was saved to rent an apartment. The leftover went for gym improvement. Over

Jack LaLanne shaking hands with Bill's long time friend, Don Farnsworth. Don was responsible for Bill opening his first gym in Sacramento, California, in 1953.

Left: Pearl's first health club in Sacramento, California, was opened in 1953, on a $2,800.00 bank account.

159

Bill Pearl's Gym was full of home built equipment. None of the members complained.

the next few years of bartering and scrimping, the gym became one of the best-equipped facilities in northern California.

My biggest profit ultimately came from selling health foods. I slowly converted the front of the gym into a well-stocked health food store by continually reinvesting, until shelves were filled with vitamins, minerals and other health-food products. Three huge glass-door refrigerators overflowed with whole grain breads, fertile eggs and certified raw-dairy products. The store, in time, paid the entire overhead of the business, which included buying the property.

During that time, Jim Drinkward and Ray Wilson had begun opening American Health/Silhouette Health Studios in several of the larger cities throughout the United States. Their clubs were equipped with mirrored walls, carpeted floors, chrome exercise equipment, childcare facilities, with many advertising indoor swimming pools and bowling alleys. It was nearly impossible for small, independent health club owners to compete against them because of their mass-marketing ability and low membership fees. (A year membership: $48.00 cash, $60.00 on installments.)

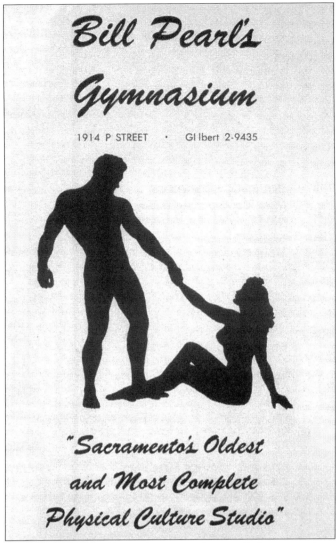

Bill Pearl's Gymnasium

1914 P STREET   ·   GIlbert 2-9435

"Sacramento's Oldest and Most Complete Physical Culture Studio"

Bill's wasn't only the oldest and most complete gym in Sacramento in 1953; it was the only gym in Sacramento.

Harold Zinkin, another individual in the fitness industry I had grown to admire, acquired a licensing agreement from American Health/Silhouette, which allowed him to open facilities under their name in scattered parts of the United States.

My early admiration for Zinkin came from the fact that he not only won the first Mr. California contest, held in 1941, but went on to win the 1945 AAU National light heavyweight Weightlifting Championships, while placing second to Clancy Ross in the AAU Mr. America contest the following day. In his spare time, Harold was a regular at Muscle Beach, performing gymnastic feats that, to many, seemed impossible. He was equally as successful in business. He and Bruce Conner opened the second health club in the Los Angeles area in 1948. Harvey Eastman had opened the first in 1947. Zinkin's club was years ahead of its time. It offered separate facilities for women and men, a special rehabilitation area; and I believe a chiropractor was on staff.

Harold established another quality health club in Fresno, California, in 1953. He also began fabricating the legendary Universal multi-station exercise machine. The machine was designed to enable several people to exercise different muscle groups at the same time. The black, five-station unit, equipped with weight stacks, sold for $1,895.00. The unit became so popular practically every health club, YMCA, and college gym in the United States purchased one. Universal Gym equipment became so popular that the name, Universal, is still what people ask for when inquiring about a multi-station unit.

Harold then commenced to open American Health/Silhouette studios throughout central California, in conjunction with his other business ventures. Zinkin approached me about opening additional clubs in northern California. I would manage the facilities and pay him a percentage of the gross receipts. It was an opportunity too good to overlook. Along with his expansions in central California, we opened two studios in Sacramento, others in Lodi and Davis, California, one in Reno, Nevada, and changed the Sacramento P-Street

Amazing does not begin to describe Harold Zinkin, a champion bodybuilder, gymnast, businessman and giver of his time to those less fortunate. Photograph taken in 1945.

Dallas Long, M.D., pressing a pair of 135-pound dumbbells.

Gym to American Health/Silhouette.

Over the next few years I paid a price for this financial success. My family life was a disaster. There weren't enough hours in the day to remember my wife and children, let alone my employees. My few workouts were being done at different YMCAs and eventually something I never thought would happen did. I quit training all together to strictly concentrate on business.

The demise of my marriage was just a part of my life's continued downward spiral. Next, American Health/Silhouette's main corporation declared bankruptcy. I found myself at the age of thirty able to put everything I valued into a cigar box and close the lid.

My way of starting over was leaving Sacramento with a stack of bills and some cash from the distress sale of the P-Street Gym. The money went as a down payment to buy George Redpath's Gym, on Manchester Boulevard in south central Los Angeles.

Redpath's Gym had been in operation since 1949. It was the first coed gym in the United States. It had a reputation for attracting all walks of life. National and Olympic track athletes, Dallas Long and Rink Babka; Jim LeFever and other great players from the Los Angeles

Harold, Bill's brother, a gym member, and Bill, in front of the Los Angeles Manchester Gym. Photograph taken in 1964.

Dodgers; world power lifting champions, Pat Casey, Bill Thurber and top athletes from the University of Southern California regularly used the facilities.

Once word spread that I had purchased the gym, it began attracting even more hard-core athletes and bodybuilders. Our mission statement should have read: Bigger and Stronger is Better. Chuck Ahrens and Steve Marjanian complained that 150-pound dumbbells weren't heavy enough. Dennis Tinerino, before winning major physique titles, left New York City to spend his summers training there. Chris Dickerson, another prize pupil, got his start at the Manchester location.

On Saturday afternoons, from 2:00-5:00, the doors were open to anyone wanting to train, free of charge. It turned the gym into an even larger three-ring circus. People came to watch; others came to impress. One monster, with hands like a Neanderthal man, challenged all-comers to a finger-pulling contest and ended up getting his finger broken. I won the 1961 and the 1967 NABBA Professional Mr. Universe titles mainly because of the intensity I trained around. You had to be good to hang with them.

Pat Casey preparing to incline press a pair of 210-pound dumbbells.

A typical Saturday morning at the Manchester Gym. Notice the rings and climbing rope hanging from the ceiling.

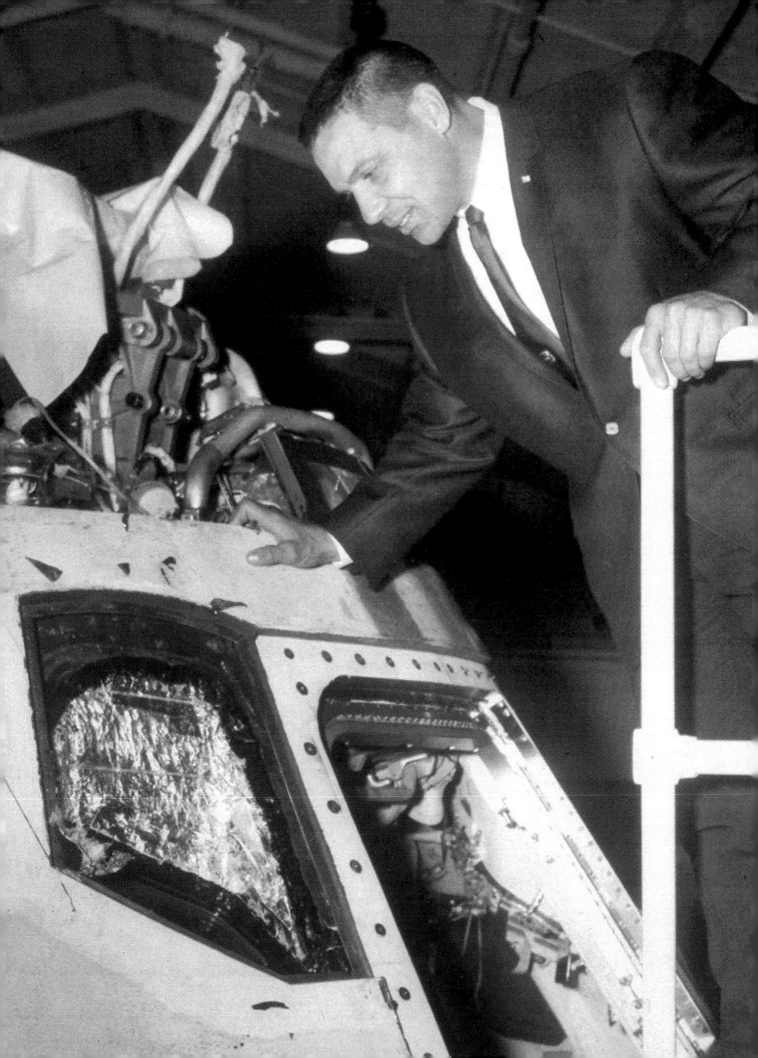

Chapter XXXII

A TIME TO CAST AWAY

If You Can Smile

If you can smile when things go wrong
And say, "It doesn't matter."
If you can laugh off care and woe
And trouble makes you fatter;

If you can keep a happy face
When all around are blue---
Then have your head examined, Bud,
There's something wrong with you!

For one thing I've arrived at:
There are no "ands" or "buts";
The guy that's grinning all the time
Must be completely nuts.

Author Unknown

Craig Whitehead, M.D., migrated from Florida to use the Los Angeles Manchester Gym, while preparing for the 1963 AAU Mr. America contest. Craig became acquainted with Harold Morrison, M.D., Chief Medical Director for North American Rockwell Corporation, the company heavily involved in the Apollo Space Program. Dr. Morrison invited Craig to their corporate office in Downey, California, to speak to the executives on the benefits of regimented exercise programs. He told them it would help curb heart attacks and reduce the high levels of stress that many of the employees were experiencing. Craig did such an excellent job that the company introduced a healthy-heart menu in the executive's dining room and set aside specific hours in their fitness facility strictly for them.

Craig recommended that Dr. Morrison hire me as a consultant to act as their personal trainer. I became a part of the program for the next ten years and was paid an hourly wage that equaled that of a practicing attorney.

Working with such an elite group broadened my scope on the health and fitness market in ways I had never considered. Physical fitness could be sold at a high cost to those who had the means and desire, but didn't have the

knowledge to succeed on their own. The Los Angeles Manchester Gym wasn't the ideal location to attract that class of clientele. It was situated on the fringes of the Watts area, which was damaged badly during the 1965 five-day race riots. Harold (my brother) and I spent five nights on the roof of the building armed with two loaded shotguns and garden hoses during that time.

Bill, Al Christensen and Craig Whitehead, M.D., in Winterhaven, Florida, in the mid-1960s.

Left: Bill consulted with the aerospace program as a personal trainer for executives and some of the astronauts for over ten years.

165

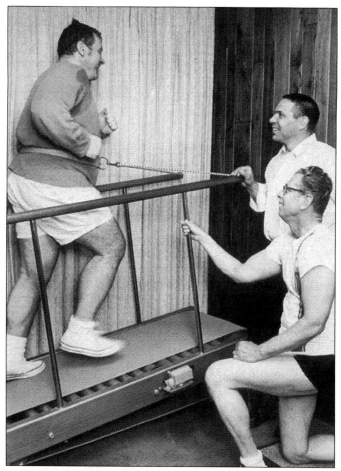

Dr. John McCarthy, President of North American Rockwell, takes a run on a manually operated treadmill, as Harold Morrison, M.D., and Bill offer encouragement.

My final decision to sell the Manchester Gym occurred while my children were visiting for a summer. Judy and I had decided to take them to an Italian restaurant close by. Three young black men proceeded to park in the space I had already two-thirds occupied. In an effort to avoid trouble, I backed our car out to give up the space. As we walked toward the restaurant one of them waited belligerently. I stopped and said, "Hey Man! You forgot to do something!" He sneered and said, "What'd I forget to do...you*&#@*^?" I said, "You forgot to thank me for the parking space." He took a swing. I knocked him to the pavement and his friends came running back to help, as all hell broke loose.

We made it to the open door of the restaurant as one of the three blacks screamed, "I live a couple of blocks from here. I'm gonna' get a gun to blow your Mother *%#*% head off!" Minutes later, with the children crying and Judy insisting that we leave, I turned to find the three standing on the sidewalk holding tire irons. With one synchronized move the tire irons were air-born. One hit in my groin area while another clipped the side of my head. Picking up the closest iron, I went after them even though

it was difficult to walk. In the short time it took us to reach our car, the parking lot had filled with a horde of blacks throwing objects. I backed the car out towards the alley just as a machete skittered across the trunk and bounced over the roof. I stopped and threw the tire iron, hoping to knock someones head off, but it bounced harmlessly on the ground.

Back at the gym the kids were still crying. Judy was nearly speechless as they went upstairs to the apartment. Harold went inside to bring out the two loaded shotguns we had used for protection during the riots. We cruised the neighborhood for hours. Thankfully, we didn't find the original three. Life was too short to do something even more stupid than I'd already done.

Bill Pearl's Manchester Gym was history. I was looking for something to do. Chuck Fish phoned, "Bill! I need your help. The Herald Examiner (one of the two daily newspapers in Los Angeles) has gone on strike. I 'gotta' get a bunch of guys together to drive strikebreakers across the picket lines. It'll be a piece of cake. All we 'gotta' do is pick'em up at a certain place, drive'em to work, and then escort'em back when their shifts are over. If anyone gives us shit we'll pound their 'friggin' heads

NASA scientist, Ray Stoddard, Bill, and Los Angeles Dodger's pitcher, Sandy Koufax, get an orientation on the material used for space flight.

166

in!" That was easy for him to say. Chuck held the World Wrestling Federation record for breaking bones and putting opponents out of commission. But, with nothing better to do with my time, and thinking the strike would probably last a few days, I said, "Why not?"

The first night on the job, a hit-and-run driver broadsided the new Pontiac station wagon I was responsible for, sending half of the passengers to the emergency room. By the end of the first week, I had changed more flat tires and cleaned more car windows than I care to remember. Unbelievably, the second week was worse. While waiting at the gate of the newspaper's parking lot, someone called out, "My God! It's Bill Pearl! Bill, roll down your window, I'm a big fan of yours." Trying to stay impartial to both sides, I did. The union worker leaned forward, spit in my face and began throwing punches.

The strike continued for months with no sign of either side giving in. All of the windows in the block-long newspaper building were bricked over. Armed guards patrolled both the outside and the inside, twenty-four hours a day. Even at home, Judy became afraid for either of us to leave our apartment.

The job came to an end on the night I dropped two non-union workers off at the Royal Motel in midtown Los Angeles. A man dressed in a long black coat stepped from a telephone booth, drew a pistol, shot both men dead, then ambled towards the station wagon.

Bill and Dr. Morrison gazing inside the Apollo 11 space capsule, after its return to earth from the moon in 1969.

Chapter XXXIII

A DREAM REALIZED

Stick To Your Task
Stick to your task till it sticks to you;
Beginners are many, but enders are few.
Honor, power, place, and praise
Will come, in time, to the one who stays.

Stick to your task till it sticks to you;
Bend at it, sweat at it, smile at it too;
For out of the bend and the sweat and the smile
Will come life's victories, after awhile.

Author Unknown

The next several months were spent traveling the Los Angeles area selling Universal Gym equipment. This was an excellent opportunity to find a location for the dream gym I had planned. A fourteen-thousand square foot, two-story building, with ample parking and a separate house on the property, became available. The location was ideal. Pasadena, California, had a population of quarter million, with the affluent neighboring cities of San Marino, South Pasadena and Sierra Madre to draw from. The location was within walking distance of the California Institute of Technology and the Pasadena City College. The competition was a YMCA and the run-down Pasadena Athletic Club.

Bill Pearl's Pasadena Health Club was a success from the opening day. The gym was divided into three separate facilities. The upstairs was for women only. The downstairs was divided into two areas where the front half was a general conditioning area, with specific hours for men and women, and the back half of the building was allocated to advanced bodybuilders. We turned one of the front offices into a health food, training and accessory store. The profits from the store paid for the building and most of the overhead.

We limited the membership of the club to one thousand yearly members. After the first year, there was a waiting list of prospective members. Our retention rate was over 80 percent. One of our best forms of advertising was the large glassed-in membership board, displaying every member's name in small white plastic letters under the month of the year he had enrolled. When the person renewed for the second year, a red dot was put after his name. Those who'd been members for five years or longer had their names displayed in gold letters. It wasn't uncommon for members who only sporadically used the club to renew their memberships just to keep their names and position on the board.

Personal trainers weren't allowed to instruct our members; instead, everyone was given special staff attention. At least one trained staff member was in each of the three areas from 8:00 a.m. to 10:00 p.m., six days a week. If a member began missing workouts, he was phoned to find out why. Special greeting cards were sent to let them know they were appreciated. We mailed monthly written reports to medical doctors and therapists who referred their patients. The adjoining lounge area had a color television with fresh coffee brewing. Lockers, towels, soap, toiletries, hair dryers, tanning beds and a shoeshine machine were available at no additional cost to the members.

It was essential for the club to have facilities for hard-core bodybuilders, if for no other reason because I needed a place to train. As much thought went into equipping that area as the rest of the gym. Many of the top bodybuilders in the Los Angeles area became members when the gym first opened; others straggled in. It wasn't long before the hard-core membership read like the

Left: Bill Pearl's Pasadena Health Club was a success from its opening day.

"Who's Who" of bodybuilding. Chris Dickerson, Jim Morris, Dr. Clint Beyerle, Dave Johns, C.F. Smith, M.D., and Bill Markakis were just a few of the more prominent bodybuilders who trained there. I looked the other way while young Bill Kazmaier (who later became the World's Strongest Man) and Dr. Sal Arria (co-founder of the ISSA Certification Course for Fitness Trainers) slipped in for periodic workouts because they couldn't afford a membership.

The club had the ability to draw from around the world. Mary Peters, accompanied by her coach, Buster McShane, came from Belfast, Northern Ireland, prior to her winning the pentathlon gold medal for Great Britain, in the 1972 Munich games. Shigeru Sugita traveled from Osaka, Japan, to spend months training at the gym preparing for the NABBA Amateur Mr. Universe, which he won in 1976. Nineteen-year-old Mr. Egypt showed up one morning carrying a small bag of clothing. "Mr. Bill

Pearl, my name is Christopher Solow. I have come from Cairo, Egypt. It has taken me two years to get here. I have worked my way from Egypt, to Lebanon, to Holland, and then to the United States, to become one of your disciples. I have no money to pay you. If you will take me on as a student I will work for you for nothing." I asked him, "Do you have a place to stay?" "No." "When did you have your last meal?" "When I left New York a few days ago." I gave him $20.00 and told him he could sleep in the gym. After following me around for a few weeks, there wasn't anything I could say or do that he couldn't do better. He became one of our most loyal employees.

We operated the club from 1968 until the end of 1979. The death of a member started me thinking more about the future than the present. It was a Monday morning. The gym was loaded with members. Don was standing at a built-in counter where training programs were filed. I asked, "How you doin' Don?" "I'm doing great Bill! Never

Jim Morris, the oldest man to win the Mr. America title at age 37. Jim competed in the 1978 Mr. Universe contest, winning his height class and second over-all at the age of 42. Jim is still a close friend of the Pearl's.

C.F. Smith, M.D., a strong competitor who could alter his body weight as much as 20 pounds over a weekend. Another of Bill's pupils.

felt better. Just got a haircut. I'm going to get in a workout before taking my lovely wife to lunch," he said.

Immediately after those words, he dropped to the floor, dead. The five medical doctors training in the gym failed to revive him. The coroner's office instructed me to cover the body and not to move it. It lay where it fell, for over six hours. During that time, at least a hundred members stepped over it and not one asked who it was or what had happened. I decided to start doing more of the things I'd been "waiting to do when I had more free time."

Dr. Clint Beyerle, former AAU Mr. USA, trained with Bill for years.

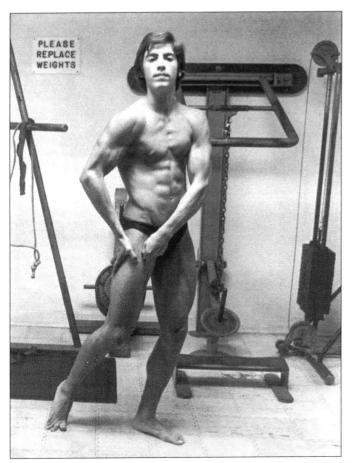

"Before and After" photographs of Doug Brignole, a member of the Pasadena Health Club, who went on to make a name for himself in the sport of bodybuilding.

171

Buster McShane and Mary Peters, who finished her training for three different Olympic games at Pearl's Gym.

Warming up with 630 pounds, Mary P was capable of an eighth-squat with 850 pounds. Bill Pearl recalled, "Mary Peters was the most powerful woman I've ever trained with."

Coach Buster McShane and Mary Peters during a training session at Bill Pearl's Pasadena Health Club, where she performed power-cleans with 225 pounds.

Ladies hours at the Pasadena Health Club.

Bill Pearls'
Keys to the INNER Universe
Worlds' best Built MAN
The most complete and comprehensive volume ever published on Body Building. Representing the knowledge gained from thirty years teaching and training Body Builders. Fully illustrated, with complete text, the Keys to Body Building and Strength are revealed through this one volume.

Chapter XXXIV

ANOTHER GOAL ACHIEVED

Books are Keys

Books are keys to wisdom's treasure:
Books are gates to lands of pleasure;
Books are paths that upward lead;
Books are friends. Come, let us read.

Author Unknown

Writing *Key's to the Inner Universe* was one of the things that I had been putting off. It became a four-year project. Two experiences (one from my youth and the other when I was an adult) are mainly responsible for the book. As a child, I often saw advertisements in magazines for the Charles Atlas training courses. In the advertisements a skinny kid was shown at the beach with his girlfriend. A big bully walking over kicked sand in the skinny boy's face, before taking the girl away. The next portion showed the 98-pound weakling with a terrific physique, simply because he had taken the Charles Atlas course. The bully was now afraid to kick sand in his face and he got his girlfriend back. During those early years, I couldn't afford the cost of the Charles Atlas program. Instead, I saved to buy a weight set. As a result I've weight trained for the past several decades.

Charles Moss, M.D., was the most influencing factor for me to write *Keys to the Inner Universe*. Dr. Moss began encouraging me to write a book on fitness when we first met, in Sacramento in 1954. After his retirement from the United States Air Force in the late 1960s, Dr. Moss became a member of our Manchester Gym in Los Angeles and continued to encourage me to get started.

It was through John Grimek that Dr. Moss and I met. Charlie had accompanied John from York, Pennsylvania, to watch our posing exhibitions at the 1954 Ed Yarick Show in Oakland, California. I recall how impressive Dr. Moss appeared in his United States Air Force uniform. His jacket was adorned with rows of medals and service ribbons, and complemented with gold clusters of a colonel pinned to his shirt collar. Fourteen years later he walked into the Manchester Gym, wearing a similar uniform, but the gold clusters were gone. Sergeant stripes

were now sewn on his sleeve.

His difficulties came while he was in charge of a large military medical hospital in Turkey. He had two major concerns for American military personnel imprisoned there. The first was his inability to get better medical treatment for them; the second, the fact that families of these servicemen were forced to raise money to ransom them to freedom.

Dr. Moss had lodged several complaints and made special trips to Washington, D.C., where it became apparent there was more concern about keeping friendly relations with the Turkish government than with the welfare of a few rowdy American servicemen. To bring this miscarriage of justice to the attention of the American people, Charlie wrote a stinging, unauthorized article that was published in a major U.S. magazine. His reward was being discharged from the United States Air Force as a

Writing *Keys to the Inner Universe* became a four-year project for Judy and Bill.

Left: Many call *Keys to the Inner Universe* the Bible of Bodybuilding.

Charlie Moss, M.D., was the influencing factor for Bill to take up writing. Dr. Moss and John Grimek's close relationship dated back to the mid-1930s.

regular, but he was allowed to finish the last few years of his career in the reserves, at a rating of Master Sergeant.

Keys to the Inner Universe had its inception one Sunday morning. Dr. Moss, Judy, and I were talking about moving from smoggy Pasadena. I had just gone through a series of tests at the University of California, Santa Barbara, to determine how a hard-core bodybuilder would compare to elite track and field athletes strictly from a health and fitness standpoint. Dr. James Wright (author of the book *Anabolic Steroids and Sports*) had conducted the study. He commented that my results would have been even better if I didn't smoke. "What are you talking about?" I said, "I haven't smoked a cigarette since I was eleven years old!" He informed me that my lungs appeared to have the damage of a two-pack-a-day smoker. We concluded that the smog backed up against the San Gabriel Mountains was the culprit.

We decided that if Judy and I were to write a complete training manual, illustrating nearly every basic exercise done with barbells/dumbbells and the most commonly used exercise machines in health clubs, and showing the beginning and ending position of each exercise, with a

brief description as to how the movements should be executed, I could act as a personal trainer anywhere in the world that had postal service (as long as everyone used the book, as a reference guide.) *Keys to the Inner Universe* grew to 648 pages and weighs over five pounds.

It took two years to photograph the beginning and ending positions of the 1,800 exercises that went into the book. Steve Green, a member of the Pasadena Health Club, came to the gym every Monday, Wednesday and Friday afternoon, to shoot photos of me doing exercises. Joan Pledger, another member, spent several hours a day for four years, hand-illustrating Steve's photographs. Harry Montgomery, also a member, gave us working space in the layout department of TypeCraft to put the book together. Four years later, as the printing press began to roll, Harry said, "Bill, I hope you know what you are doing. You're going to have so much money into this project, you'll never get it back." My reply was, "Harry, don't you worry about it. All we have to do is sell 50,000 copies. We'll be fine."

The first copy of the book went to Dr. Moss. We had spent over $250,000.00, without having a clue what to do with the 9,999 copies stored at TypeCraft. My first thought was to get expert marketing advice. My immediate thoughts turned to Joe Weider. Joe took several minutes to scan the book before commenting, "Here's what I would do. I'd carry a copy wherever I went and show the book to everyone that I came into contact with. When it got to the point where it started to make me puke to talk about it, I'd know I was making progress."

The next call went to Arthur Jones. I flew to Slidell, Louisiana, to spend two days and nights at his home listening to him talk about everything BUT the book. He had tossed his autographed copy on a table, never bothering to leaf through it. On the third day, I grew tired of his bullshit and said, "Arthur, you know why I'm here. I want your advice on how to market my book." He looked at me as if I was the most stupid person on earth and replied, "ADVERTISE, you silly bastard! ADVERTISE!" I called a cab and left for the airport.

We began doing everything we could imagine to market the book: running $5,000.00 half-page, color ads in *Muscle and Fitness*, sending copies to the editors of the other major physique magazines. We visited health clubs, providing them with displays and leaving copies on consignment. We set up a booth at every fitness, sporting goods or bodybuilding show of consequence. Often our friend, Tom Lincir of Ivanko Barbell, shared his booth with us.

Within the first year we were averaging $40,000.00 a month in sales out of the house on the Pasadena Health Club's property. At any given time, there were two to three thousand copies of our book stored in the house, along with packaging and shipping materials. It was like a maze, getting from the front to the back. There was only room to eat and sleep, while trucks kept coming to either deliver or to pick up shipments.

Once distribution began, I started inserting into each book a flyer and a comprehensive feedback sheet stating that Bill Pearl would personally train a select number of students via mail. All the individual had to do was "fill out the following information and immediately return it to Bill Pearl's Physical Fitness Architects." We were averaging fifty letters a day with the filled-out information, along with checks or money orders to cover the cost. The volume of requests became impossible to

Betty and Joe Weider pose for photograph with Bill. Joe has been a big supporter of Bill for over fifty years.

control. There weren't enough hours in the day to sell the book and handle the personal training, let alone run the gym.

Twenty-five years later, the book is still averaging sales of 10,000 copies per year in the United States alone. It has been translated into German, Italian, Danish and Spanish. I'm still using the marketing tool that was suggested by Joe Weider. I carry a copy when speaking to audiences who are involved in fitness and give the book away as a gift. I do this by ending my presentation saying, "I have brought a gift for someone. To be fair, and to give everyone a chance, I'm going to ask a question. The first person to answer the question correctly will receive this book as a gift. (I then hold the book up.) If someone can tell me the author of the best book ever written on resistance weight training, this book, *Keys to the Inner Universe*, is yours!" The name "Bill Pearl" rings throughout the audience.

"If someone can tell me the author of the best book on weight training... and I'm not looking for the name Arnold Schwarzenegger... this book, *Keys to the Inner Universe*, is yours as a gift."

This page has been intentionally left blank.

Chapter XXXV

WHEN WILL WE LEARN?

As A Man Soweth
We must not hope to be mowers,
And to gather the ripe gold ears,
Unless we have first been sowers
And watered the furrows with tears.
It is not just as we take it,
This mystical world of ours,
Life's field will yield as we make it
A harvest of thorns or flowers.

Johnann Wolfgang Van Goethe

As previously mentioned, the names Pearl and Stern became synonymous in the bodybuilding world for twenty years, much the same as ham and eggs or barbells and dumbbells. We collaborated on numerous business ventures. One of the first items we marketed was a form-fit T-shirt made by a company that Leo and George Redpath owned and operated. Next came a line of posing briefs in a variety of styles and colors. The briefs were manufactured exclusively for us by Elon of California, a San Diego-based company owned by Haydon Tallieffero, a friend and bodybuilding enthusiast.

Then, in the early 1960s, Leo and I put together a series of training booklets: *Building Bulk and Power, Complete Chest Development, Fabulous Forearms, Your Key to Broad Shoulders* and *Build Big Arms.* Countless thousands were sold through small ads in major physique magazines. Following our example, Vince Gironda, Reg Park, Larry Scott, Arnold Schwarzenegger, Chuck Sipes, Frank Zane and others produced training courses of their own.

T-shirts remained a big seller. In 1976 we produced the Bicentennial Stars and Stripes "All American." It continued to sell long after the two hundredth birthday of the United States.

Within our Pasadena Health Club, Judy and I operated a small health food store that carried the most popular brands of products, mainly formulated for elite athletes. Among our best selling products was a line

called "Scientific Nutrition." John Balik, now better known as the publisher of *Iron Man* magazine, was a major distributor of the line.

For several years, I had "Scientific Nutrition" products privately labeled under Physical Fitness Architects and continued to sell them through mail order and Bill Pearl Enterprises, our Phoenix, Oregon-based fitness store.

In the late 1970s, we were approached by a group of attorneys regarding a new business venture. They planned to offer a licensing agreement to anyone wanting to open health clubs in the United States and Canada. If agreed, the gyms would be called Bill Pearl's Fitness Plus.

Leo and Bill sold countless thousands of their training booklets before other champion bodybuilders began to saturate the market.

Left: Richard Hadder, Dave Johns, Bill, and Jim Morris celebrate the two hundredth birthday of the United States of America by wearing Bill's "All American" T-shirt.

For the use of our name, Judy and I were to receive stock in the corporation, in addition to a percentage of the gross receipts from the clubs. It sounded too good to be true. It was. We should have walked away.

Bill Pearl's Fitness Plus began advertising the sale of the licensing agreement. The number of takers and inquiries were surprising. As the business grew, the attorneys suggested that we take a more active role in the overall operation. To show good faith, we were asked to purchase additional stock and sit on the board of directors. Two years later, there were sixty-nine health clubs using the name Bill Pearl's Fitness Plus. Like an idiot, I convinced Judy that we should leave our percentage of the gross receipts on the books to help with company expansion.

In its third year, Bill Pearl's Fitness Plus applied to the attorney general's office of the state of California to be granted a permit to offer a franchise rather than a licensing agreement to anyone in California. The idea was to start franchising gyms in California and then expand to other states, while offering the licensing agreement until this took place. Our corporate office in the Orange County area of southern California staffed twenty to twenty-five people who took care of the daily operations, telemarketing and advertising, and ran the week-long training school gym owners and staff were required to attend.

In 1982, the economy of the U.S. took a downturn. Some of the newer operations had difficulty meeting their obligations to Bill Pearl's Fitness Plus. They were told by the operation officer to take out loans and borrow on their homes and cars, or were threatened with lawsuits. New prospects considering getting involved with the company were being badgered to death. It became apparent that well-meaning people, not in a financial position to wait out the storm, were being pushed into making business decisions that could jeopardize not only them, but also their immediate families.

The financial picture of the U.S. remained stagnant. Finally, at a quarterly board meeting, Judy and I stated our concerns, then resigned from the board of directors. We also declined to renew the agreement that allowed the corporation to use the name Bill Pearl. Lawsuits were immediately filed by some of the gym owners against the Florida-based corporation.

Even though our main office was in California, most of the board of directors of Bill Pearl's Fitness Plus had no tangible assets in California. Judy and I lived in California

with assets that could be attached. The judge ruled in favor of one defendant, but thankfully didn't award the million dollars the defendant was suing for. However, the judge did pierce the corporate code and ruled that Judy and I personally pay back all franchise fees. By the time the suits were settled, the only things we had to show for our efforts were more gray hair and diminishing trust in our fellow man.

Again in 1982, Herman Lewis, a biochemist, and owner of Shamrock Labs in Dublin, California, approached me with the idea of a Bill Pearl's Championship Nutrition line, which included over sixty different products.

The line was distributed through health food stores, super markets, sporting goods chains and health clubs and sold extremely well as long as I remained visible in the fitness industry.

After many years of ups, downs and frustration at the mercy of vendors who went out of business, made radical changes in pricing, or otherwise changed the game plan, Judy and I decided that we did the best with things we could produce ourselves. Our books have proven that people were searching for information and variety in their exercise regimen. I designed a series of training program cards and posters, depicting numerous choices to help with program changes essential to maintaining interest and results. We promote them on our website www.billpearl.com in two series: a home series using barbells, dumbbells and a minimum of home equipment, and a pro-series, consisting of nine posters, each devoted to a body part and using commercial gym equipment.

Always looking for new projects and challenges, I imagine I'll continue to search for the "goose that laid the golden egg" until they close the lid on the box.

THE ART
OF
POSING

BY
LARRY SCOTT

arnold:
developing a mr. universe physique

Examples of the training booklets offered by other legendary bodybuilders... Larry Scott, Arnold Schwarzenegger, Chuck Sipes and Frank Zane, to name a few.

HOW
TO
PLAN
YOUR
BODYBUILDING
TRAINING

by
Chuck
Sipes

How To
Develop
Championship
Legs
And A
Small
Waistline

by
FRANK
ZANE

Chapter XXXVI

A SAD FAREWELL

People Liked Him

People liked him, not because
He was rich or known to fame;
He had never won applause
As a star in any game.
His was not a brilliant style;
His was not a forceful way.
But he had a gentle smile
And kindly word to say.

Edgar A. Guest

Judy and I began commuting from Pasadena to our small ranch in southern Oregon, one week each month, in 1975. Our first project was to convert our large barn into a private gym. A select group of friends were invited to use the facility and it has remained that way.

John McGinnis (a gym owner and physique promoter) from Derby, England, came to visit during part of his trip through the United States. He convinced me to give a posing exhibition at the 1987 Derby Classic. I promised myself and everyone I cared for, this would be the last time I'd be seen in public in a pair of posing briefs.

During the time between John's Oregon visit and my 1987 commitment, McGinnis contracted stomach cancer. In Oregon he was full of life, but by the time Judy and I arrived in England, he was barely holding on. Yet, he was insistent that the contest not be canceled and was adamant about introducing me onstage.

It became apparent that John had been too sick to properly promote the contest. The NABBA Mr. Universe contest was taking place the weekend before the Derby Classic. I thought if I volunteered to give a free posing exhibition at their contest, it would draw attention to John's. They declined my offer. One promoter said, "It's not worth our time having you onstage, but we will make an announcement that you will be posing at John's show the following weekend." In the matter of a few short years, I'd gone from being one of the highest paid modern bodybuilders giving exhibitions to offering to pose for nothing.

The day of the Derby Classic wasn't what we had imagined. John was lying on the floor of his office trying to conserve strength. By 4:00 p.m. he had become comatose and was rushed to the hospital. Just before the show's curtains opened, we phoned to inform his wife that it was a full house. She replied, "I just told John. He whispered 'Thank you,' then closed his eyes and died."

Left: Bill conducting a seminar in Derby, England, in 1987. He promised himself this would be the last time he would appear in public in a pair of posing briefs.

Photographs of Bill taken in Derby, England, thirty-four years after winning his first NABBA Mr. Universe title.

This page has been intentionally left blank.

Chapter XXXVII

NEW BEGINNINGS

Pass It On
Have you had a kindness shown?
Pass it on.

'Twas not given for thee alone.
Pass it on.

Let it travel down the years,
Let it wipe another's tears,
Till in heaven the deed appears.
Pass it on.

Henry Burton

The first year in Oregon was terrific. Building the home gym, working out six days a week, remodeling other structures on the property and mowing acres of weeds kept us busy. Then boredom set in.

We purchased a piece of commercial real estate in the small town of Phoenix, Oregon (just on the outskirts of Medford). We established Bill Pearl Enterprises, a general fitness store that sold weightlifting equipment and nutritional supplements. Our mail order business, which included book sales, was moved to the new location. This gave us more to do each day than we could get done. Shortly after, Lloyd Kahn (owner of Shelter Publications, publisher of Bob Anderson's best seller *Stretching* and of Jeff Galloway's *Book on Running*) contacted us. Lloyd had seen *Keys to the Inner Universe* while visiting Bob Anderson. He wanted to publish a smaller and more mainstream version of the book.

Getting Stronger was published in 1986. It has become one of the best selling books written on resistance weight training. It has been translated into four languages, with sales of over 600,000 copies in North America and a million worldwide. Twenty-four of the country's top coaches, trainers and athletes (including two world-record holders and eleven Olympic coaches) helped in developing the strength training programs featured in the book.

Regardless of the success of *Getting Stronger*, *Keys to*

the Inner Universe remains my favorite. It continues to sell at a surprising rate for the reason that over the past three decades, exercise machines have become so popular most people have forgotten how to use free weights. Those who are looking for the best reference guide to incorporate free weights back in their training regimen have little choice but to turn to *Keys to the Inner Universe*.

Keys to the Inner Universe remains Pearl's favorite. "Those looking for the best free-weights reference have little choice but to turn to this book."

Left: Pearl plays farmer.

Chapter XXXVIII

WHEN OPPORTUNITY KNOCKS

Three Things Come Not Back
Remember three things come not back:
The arrow sent upon its track---
It will not swerve, it will not stay
Its speed; it flies to wound, or slay.
The spoken word so soon forgot
By thee; but it has perished not;
In other hearts 'tis living still
And doing work for good or ill.
And the lost opportunity
That cometh back no more to thee,
In vain thou sweepest, in vain dost yearn,
Those three will nevermore return.

Author Unknown

"Hello, Bill, this is Paul Ward. We used to train together at Stern's Gym nearly forty years ago. Do you remember me?" How could I have forgotten Paul? He had played professional football, obtained a Ph.D, coached at several colleges, acted as an Olympic athletic trainer and was still winning Master's National Power-Lifting Championships. He also conducted numerous research studies on all aspects of weight training. "I'm working as a consultant for Life Fitness and Health and Tennis, the chain of fitness centers. We're designing a new line of computerized strength training machines called Lifecircuit®. I'd like to send you some information to obtain your input."

He described Lifecircuit® as if the concepts were new, yet his comments were surprisingly similar to those Judy and I had heard from Arthur Jones in the early 1970s. "The machines offer the user a set-up test that automatically determines the correct weight to begin an exercise. The resistance can be increased, or decreased, just by pressing a button. In addition, you can automatically increase the negative resistance of the eccentric part of the movement. Here's what I'm talking about. Let's use a barbell curl as an example. The positive movement, known as concentric, occurs when you curl a

barbell to shoulder height. The negative motion, known as eccentric, happens while lowering the barbell back to

Dr. Paul Ward played professional football, coached at several colleges, acted as an Olympic athletic trainer and still found time to consult with major exercise equipment manufacturers.

Left: Augie Nieto, former President of Life Fitness, Inc., kept Pearl in the public's eye by involving him in the promotion of their fitness products. Bill is still consulting for the company.

191

Ken Germano was mainly responsible for Pearl going to work with Life Fitness, in 1986. Bill is still traveling worldwide for the company.

arm's length. In theory, if a person is capable of curling 100 pounds to shoulder height, then that person is capable of correctly lowering 140 pounds back to the starting position. Our new machines are the only ones that have the built-in capabilities to do this. If you don't want to use an additional negative workload, press another button which will cause the workload for the positive (concentric) and negative (eccentric) to become the same as if you were using free-weights or standard exercise machines."

I asked, "How difficult is it for someone like me, who is not comfortable pushing buttons, to program machines? And another thing, do they have the feel of barbells and dumbbells?" "That's the main reason for the call. If you like what's in the information, we want to invite you to Irvine, California, to train on the equipment. Hopefully you'll give us feedback before we introduce the "circuit" to the members of Health and Tennis."

The conversation with Paul convinced me that the Lifecircuit® machines had a potential to revolutionize the fitness industry. Their unique features accommodated the needs of people from beginning to advanced bodybuilders and those working with injuries, teaching people how to exercise correctly, while helping to eliminate the need for personal instructions.

Paul phoned again a few days later. "We're on our way to Oregon. I'm bringing Ken Germano, the marketing director of Life Fitness, with me." When they arrived, Ken left most of the conversation to Paul. Ken seemed more interested in my work schedule and if I had the time and enthusiasm to assist with the promotion of the new product line.

I made the trip to Irvine to train on the prototype machines. Speaking with Augie Nieto, president of Life Fitness, I commented, "Your new machines could have a larger impact on the fitness industry than Universal or Nautilus!" He smiled and asked, "Would you like to come to work for us?" My reply was, "No! Not unless I have every piece of the new line in my barn to train on."

Our barn was transformed into one of the most high-tech fitness facilities in the state of Oregon. Everyone using the "circuit" became a part of an experiment. The gamut ran from 80-year-old neighbors to former Mr. Olympia winner Chris Dickerson. We began using the machines for pre-exhaustion training, negative-only training and super-setting, along with incorporating them into programs with standard weight equipment and free weights.

I designed training programs based on the records that I kept, to demonstrate the unique versatility of the equipment. Nobody from Life Fitness questioned me on my presentation of the line. In fact, Life Fitness hasn't questioned me on anything I've done for the company over the past two decades. Their confidence in me has been one of my biggest motivators for not retiring.

Here is a side note that may benefit up-and-coming bodybuilders who have hopes of finding a career in the fitness industry. At the same time Life Fitness approached me, they also approached Lee Haney, who was, at that time, the current and several times Mr. Olympia winner. The plan was to match Lee Haney (the young bull) with Bill Pearl (the old bull). I had the greatest respect for Lee and was looking forward to working with him. I later heard that Lee's business manager had asked for a huge sum of up-front money to get him involved. Augie Nieto (president of Life Fitness) said, "NO!"

Years later, while in Atlanta, Georgia, I stopped by Lee Haney's gym. He asked, "Are you still working for Life Fitness?" The old bull had to speak up, "Yes!" I said. "And I'd like to share something with you that may be helpful in the future. Back in 1988, the amount of money your manager asked Life Fitness for, and you didn't receive--I did. It just took me longer to get it." The point being: I felt Lee had passed up the opportunity to work for the greatest exercise equipment manufacturer in the world. Instead of looking at the big picture and the potential benefits of association, the individual Lee had relied on simply looked for the "quick buck" as the bottom line. In reality, what Lee passed up were dividends that would have continued long after people had forgotten the number of times he had won the Mr. Olympia contest. My length of time working for Life Fitness is proof. I still act as a spokesperson promoting the company by traveling hundreds of thousands of miles each year. The most exciting thing for me is seeing so many of the young people, who were a part of the original team, still with the company and now filling executive roles.

Inside view of Bill's high-tech home gym, better known as the "Barn."

Arnold and Augie discuss business tactics, as Bill keeps his back to the camera to show off his bald spot. He later commented, "It's the only thing besides my waist that continues to grow."

Lee Haney reigned as "King" in the sport of bodybuilding for over ten years and is still considered one of the greatest. He continues to practice what he preaches.

Bill's relationship with Life Fitness requires him to travel as much as 200,000 miles each year.

Augie arranged for a high school marching band and cheerleaders to help celebrate Pearl's 65th birthday at a major fitness trade show in Chicago. Lou Ferrigno did the honors, acting as the Master of Ceremonies.

Lou Ferrigno and Augie Nieto embarrassing Bill during a National Trade Show on his 65th birthday.

Chapter XXXIX

THE INNER SELF

Answer To Prayer
We ask for strength and God Gives us difficulties which make us strong.
We pray for wisdom and God sends us problems,
The solution of which develops wisdom.
We plead for prosperity and God gives us dangers to overcome.
We ask for favors---God gives us opportunities.
This is the answer.

Author Unknown

My father had mixed emotions about Christianity. He felt it was largely responsible for the demise of the Native Americans. Nothing anyone could say would alter this belief. There may have been a slight change in dad's attitude during my parent's older years, when they became involved in the Church of Latter-Day Saints.

As previously mentioned, I regularly attended church services during junior and senior high school. The last two years of my military enlistment I joined a Bible study group. I spent hours reading the Bible, (both testaments), the Talmud, the Book of Mormon and the Testimony of Buddha. Comparing each to the other, I attempted to better understand the different philosophies. This resulted in me NOT becoming a better Christian--just more confused as to what is right and what is wrong.

A young woman came to our fitness store in 1985, dressed in a sari. She introduced herself as Kelly Chamblis, but preferred to be called by her Sanskrit name, Mandahbi. (The name given to her by her spiritual teacher, Sri Chinmoy.) Mandahbi had recently attended a large world peace concert organized by Guru Sri Chinmoy and his followers in New York City. She learned that Guru had just taken up weight training and mentioned that she lived close to our business. Guru apparently knew of my background and asked if I would answer some basic questions regarding his strength training. Her first visit lasted fifteen minutes. A few days later, she was back asking more questions and taking notes.

After several very pleasant meetings, Judy and I

became curious. We began asking questions about Sri Chinmoy. The more we learned, the more fascinated we became. We discovered he is best known for his peace meditations at the United Nations, his concerts, and his literary and artistic achievements. He has written over fifteen hundred books, painted millions of pictures, and plays numerous musical instruments. Guru expects his disciples to be nearly as active in their own way. His followers operate several spiritual centers and varied business ventures around the world, attempting to promote world peace through non-violent efforts.

For the next several months, we stayed in touch with Guru mainly through Mandahbi, as I continued to play the role of weightlifting coach. In late June of 1986, we were invited, along with other world champion bodybuilders, weightlifters, Olympians, dignitaries and students, to attend a large gathering in Jamaica, New York, to celebrate the first anniversary of Sri Chinmoy's weightlifting career. Carl Lewis and Al Oerter were guests, along with Terry and Jan Todd, both world champion power lifters.

Guru and a group of his students met the two of us at the La Guardia International Airport. Our first impression, especially of Guru, was overwhelming. The kindness in all of their hearts was obvious; yet, as they walked toward us, an aura of light appeared to surround Guru. His first words were, "Oh my, Bill and Judy Pearl! I've been waiting years for this! I've finally gotten to meet you. I have respected Bill since I was a young boy, living in India. I think of him as my soul brother. I am so happy

Left: Seventy-one-year old Sri Chinmoy being congratulated by seventy-two-year old Bill, after performing feats of strength Bill would not have attempted in his youth.

Sri Chinmoy welcoming Bill and Judy to Jamaica, New York, to celebrate the first anniversary of Guru's weightlifting career in 1986.

Bill and Judy with good friends and Sri Chinmoy devotees, Ashrita Ferman and Abakash Konapiaty.

WEIGHT 403
APP. 50
TOTAL 453

"Two most precious Pearls" according to Sri Chinmoy.

to finally get to meet you both in person. Thank you so much for coming."

Ashrita Furman and Abakash Konapiaty were assigned as guides for our stay in New York. Abakash is an avid weightlifting enthusiast, along with owning a modern printing facility in the New York City area. Ashrita has the ability, plus the energy, to have held seventy-four of the records found in the *Guinness Book of Records*. Both are extremely intelligent, patient and completely devoted to Sri Chinmoy. Like all of his students, they give credit to Guru for their inspiration to attempt to make a positive difference.

From the airport we were driven to a five-star hotel, handed the key to a room decorated with bouquets of flowers, a large basket of fruit, and given time to freshen up. Later, Abakash drove us to a vegetarian restaurant owned by another of Guru's students. Guru sat at our table and talked mostly about my bodybuilding accomplishments and seldom referred to himself. His only spiritual comment was that he constantly prayed for a oneness-world filled with God-loving people. Those sitting close by were particularly eager to hear what Guru had to say and listened to every word.

Nearly a thousand people attended the evening performance. A mixed choir opened the presentation by singing East Indian spiritual songs that Guru had composed. Through the four-hour marathon, Guru performed one feat of strength after another, never failing to complete an attempt. The total amount of weight he lifted that evening was 157,000 pounds. Two of the feats I remember clearly were of him supporting 1,700 pounds on his shoulders and then doing a partial calf-raise. The other was to raise two 500-pound dumbbells, held in racks a few inches below arm's length, and support them overhead. Making this even more difficult to believe was that Guru was fifty-four years old, weighed 148 pounds and had seriously weight trained for only sixteen months.

During a short break in his performance, I was asked to come onstage to demonstrate a standing-side-lateral-raise (a movement Guru felt may help improve his shoulder strength). I demonstrated the exercise and then handed the pair of 10-pound dumbbells to him. After completing three repetitions, he stopped and said in a loud voice, "This is too heavy. I can't do this." I was shocked! All evening Guru had lifted weights that I would never attempt, yet, when it came to Sri Chinmoy--his

Sri Chinmoy raised 1,700 pounds using a standing calf-raise machine on 31 October 1986.

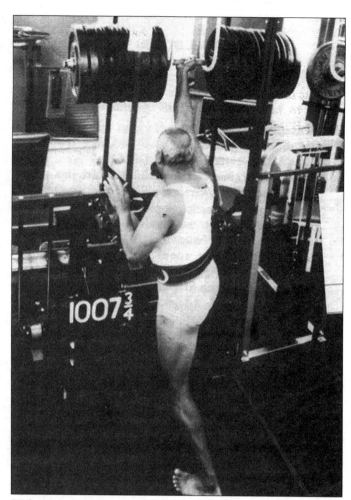

With one arm, Sri Chinmoy lifted 1,007 3/4 pounds, more than six times his body weight, on 10 November 1986.

outer person--10-pound dumbbells were too heavy.

Time didn't seem to enter into the equation. It was well past midnight before several hundreds of his followers traveled to another location to be fed and to listen to Guru play musical instruments and sing spiritual songs that were foreign to my ears.

Soon after Judy and I returned home, articles and photographs of Guru began appearing in fitness magazines. It was mentioned that I was one of the guests who had witnessed the lifting event. Some of the phone calls and letters I received were to question the legitimacy of what had been written, especially the pressing of two 500-pound dumbbells; also the 1700-pound standing-calf-raise. My response was, "I saw him stand erect with the 1700 pounds on his shoulders and do what could be considered a partial calf-raise. Regarding the 500-pound dumbbells--Guru did not press the weight overhead; he supported the weight overhead at arm's length."

Terry Todd (a true historian on weight training) had also witnessed the lifts and apparently became determined to set the records straight. His written rebuttal as to what actually took place brought additional publicity for Guru. It was not the type of publicity either Guru or anyone who loves and respects him was looking for. With the hopes of putting an end to the negative publicity, I volunteered to edit future articles on his lifting events to make sure the lifts were described in more accurate terminology.

Guru continued to handle heavier weight in manners that were not considered traditional in the weightlifting world. This seemed to cause more confusion among the die-hard bodybuilders and weightlifters because he wasn't squatting, pressing, snatching, cleaning, or dead-lifting.

In November of 1986, I received a photo of Guru standing under a dumbbell weighing an incredible 1007 3/4 pounds. The dumbbell was supported on a rack just short of Guru's overall height. Several of his disciples swore Guru had raised the weight and supported it at arm's length for the briefest period of time. What astonished me, even more than the horrendous weight, was that Guru completed the lift using one arm! It was beyond my comprehension that anyone could have that amount of faith to believe such a feat was humanly possible.

I telephoned Guru, to congratulate him while suggesting that the photo not be published. I was afraid that--like in the past--it would cause more bad publicity. It was published and my assumptions were correct. My defense for Guru was, "Regardless of whether it is true, or not, doesn't alter my respect and admiration for Sri Chinmoy. Anyone with such conviction and inner faith to believe they are capable of such an amazing feat deserves all of our respect and admiration."

I later commented to Guru that the average person who wasn't a weightlifter couldn't understand the difference between objects weighing 500 pounds to those weighing 2000 pounds. To them they were just numbers. But by lifting objects the general population could better relate to, such as automobiles, large animals, or platforms of people, then nobody would question how the lifts were done or how much the objects weighed. He took my advice and added those types of feats to his lifting events. The outcome was nothing but praise and additional amazement from those who attended his events.

Judy and I attended Guru's World Peace Concert in 1988. We were offered the Sanskrit names of: Bhavatarini Judy Pearl and Mahasamrat Bill Pearl. We gratefully accepted the compliment and began using the names in conversations, and events in association with Guru and his students. Over the years our Sanskrit names have become even more special as we have grown to learn the love that goes with them.

Our relationship grew even stronger during the 1990s. I began acting as Master of Ceremonies for Guru's special lifting events. On November 17, 1999, a celebration of his 14th weightlifting anniversary was held at York College in Jamaica, New York. The auditorium was filled with dignitaries and world-class athletes from around the world. I began the evening by saying; "It is my pleasure to welcome you to the Sri Chinmoy fitness marathon. This evening you are going to see some amazing feats of strength performed by a sixty-eight year old man weighing 167 pounds. In no way do I classify this person as a world's strongest man; I think of him as a world-class religious leader. Today you are going to see some amazing feats of strength that I myself--and I have been in the industry for fifty-five years--would not even attempt to

Minnie, the thirty year old Asian elephant, obligingly received Mahasamrat Bill Pearl as a rider, while she patiently waited to be lifted a few inches off the ground by Sri Chinmoy.

Bill commented to Guru, Sri Chinmoy, that the average person who wasn't a weightlifter couldn't understand the difference between an object weighing 500 pounds and those weighing 2,000 pounds.

"I have no idea how far my Lord will carry me. Whatever goal he has set for me, most devotedly I shall follow him. His compassion and guidance are my outer strength and inner power."

Sri Chinmoy

perform. I seriously doubt that any top athlete in the world would attempt to duplicate what you are going to see. I believe you are in for a big surprise at what a small man with a gigantic heart and soul can accomplish."

The audience was not disappointed. Guru performed sixty-five different feats, which included lifting four grand pianos that were placed on a platform. He continued to please his fans and loyal students by lifting several guests ranging from the one-hundred-ten year old Hindu spiritual leader, Swami Bua-ji, to Monsignor Thomas Hartman. (Guru's close friend for nearly twenty years) Closing the event, I followed Guru to center stage where I extended his right arm, as the audience stood to applaud his efforts. He remarked, "I have no idea how far my Lord will carry me. Whatever goal he has set for me, most devotedly I shall follow. His compassion and guidance are my outer strength and my inner power."

I had the privilege to be part of another lifting event performed by Guru in late 2002. He continues to conduct peace concerts throughout the world, drawing crowds numbering in the thousands and continues to meet with dignitaries and high-ranking public officials from different countries to promote world peace through non-violent efforts. If I may use myself as a testimonial, Sri Chinmoy and his students have been tremendously successful. For the past seventeen years, they have brought a world of peace into Judy's and my life through their non-violent loving efforts. I find myself no longer questioning what is right and what is wrong. That decision has been left to God.

All supporters of Sri Chinmoy, from left to right, Mike Katz, Bill, Wayne DeMilia, Sri Chinmoy and Frank Zane.

203

IN CONCLUSION

Growing Smiles
A smile is quite a funny thing,
It wrinkles up your face,
And when it's gone, you never find
It's secret hiding place.

But far more wonderful it is
To see what smiles can do;
You smile at one, he smiles at you,
And so one smile makes two.

He smiles at someone since you smiled,
And then that one smiles back;
And that one smiles, until in truth
You fail in keeping track.

Now since a smile can do great good
By cheering hearts of care,
Let's smile and smile and not forget
That smiles go everywhere!

Author Unknown

As a youth, it bothered me to think that people were laughing at seeing my weaknesses and imperfections. I thought that by becoming big and powerful enough to defend myself, it would make my problems and insecurities disappear. Attempting to achieve this goal has taken so much time, effort and focus that other aspects of my life have suffered.

Always watching people and observing what works for them has been a part of my life. Curiosity and analysis were major reasons for my success. In early childhood, curiosity and analysis came in the form of emulating the people who had the success I wanted. In my pre-teens it was a circus strongman. After my sister gave me my first subscription to a physique magazine, it became John Grimek. In high school, it was Norm Burke, my wrestling coach. As an adult, I turned to Leo Stern. Each held slightly different qualities that I wanted for myself.

As a youth, Bill was concerned that people were seeing his weaknesses and imperfections.

Left: Bill's closing remarks, "I am a victim of habit. I love knowing what I am going to do day-in and day-out, but still I remain the same inquisitive kid who wondered what was in all the old barns I could not see into."

Still Sizzling at 63

At the age of 63, veteran bodybuilder B I L L PEARL is a living proof that nutritious eating and weight training, rather than Ponce de Leon's legendary Fountain of Youth, can stave off the debilitating effects of old age.

'I'm probably as enthusiastic today as I was in 1953 when I began competitive bodybuilding in San Diago, California,' explains Pearl. 'I still train six days a week, three hours a day, from 3,30 to 6,30 am.

Born in Prineville, Oregan, and reared in Yakima, Washington, Bill Pearl was **Mr. America in 1953, Mr. U.S.A. in 1956, and Mr. Universe in 1953,1956, 1961, 1967, and 1971.**

His training is a modified version of 40 years ago. 'I just don't handle as much heavy weight as I used to. I don't care if I can bench press 400 lbs for one repetition or five any more, because I've found that if I do get an injury it just takes forever to heal. I still handle relatively heavy weights, but I train faster with the same amount of intensity.'

Pearl also limits the amount of animal fats and refined sugar in his diet, as excess amounts of both have been proven to cause obesity and illness. Ironically it was an inferiority complex that first motivated him to weight train.

'When I was 11 years old I weighed 111 lbs, but I had a size seven and five eighths inch head,' Pearl

20

SIXTY SOMETHING – SOMETHING SEXY.

Bill commented, "I plan to continue weight training until they put the lid on my coffin."

With the time and effort that has gone into making my career, two positives come to mind. I have earned financial security and a reasonable amount of fame. Much of my financial success has come from investing in commercial real estate. In every business I've owned, I've purchased the property.

Yet, fame has brought some disappointment. For the large part, professional bodybuilding is synonymous with the word "freak." The result for me has been concealing what I have spent most of my life trying to achieve, by wearing baggy clothing and taking my shirt off in public only when required as part of being a professional bodybuilder. When the job was done, I'd go back into hiding.

The feeling of being an outsider has always made me cheer for the underdogs. My wish is always to see them beat the odds. I've learned through trial and error that you can better your chances of winning by being friendly and having a positive attitude. It also helps to zero in on people's names and use eye contact. Being a good listener and wearing a winning smile also knocks down barriers. This is particularly true of the smile. If you smile at a group of three, the odds are that all three will smile back.

I've tried to remain cordial to most everybody. I want to be noted as a nice person who is self-reliant and doesn't depend on anybody other than his immediate family. I don't want anything given to me, nor do I want anybody hindering my progress. I'm more serious than jovial. If someone showers me with gratitude, I become nervous. I have very few "best friends," a lot of "friends," and a ton of "acquaintances." I am a victim of habit. I love knowing what I am going to do day-in and day-out, and I still remain the same inquisitive kid who wondered what was in all the old barns I could not see into.

Along the way, I've discovered that although being big and powerful doesn't earn you respect or acceptance, it may give you the self-respect and confidence to expect to be treated the way you treat others. For me, acceptance has come to mean being appreciated for what I am.

Bill, Spencer and Phil: Three generations of Pearls.

YOU HAVE REACHED THE OFFICE OF BILL PEARL

Bill stated in chapter five that if you were to visit his office you would find no trophies, but a huge glass jar filled with two thousand marbles, which he has saved since childhood. This may have given you an indication that he is an avid collector. He collected antique automobiles and home furnishing until we ran out of space in our home and garages. Now he fills his office with a collection of scale-model cars, trucks, airplanes, and bicycles, as well as antique bicycles, toys, lamps, etc. They give his office a sense of history, which he enjoys. The following pages are a sample of a few of the items in his collection.

Judy Pearl

Bill working at one of his work stations.

Left: Welcome to the office of Bill and Judy Pearl.

Another view of Bill's office featuring a restored 1875 Columbia Pope high-wheel bicycle. Bill has ridden and fallen off this bicycle more than once.

Bill smiles while holding a wooden dumbbell, with an antique arcade strength machine waiting to challenge him.

The most commonly asked question by people visiting Pearl's office is, "Where did all this stuff come from?"

An antique wind-up toy tricycle. (Something for everyone!)

Every day seems like Christmas in Bill's office, which is more like an antique Toys 'R' Us store.

A Tinkham 1895 three-wheel bicycle.

An 1898 Rambler bicycle equipped with wooden rims. The Rambler bicycle was the beginning of the Nash Rambler automobile.

Bill's current collection of restored antique and classic automobiles has leveled off at thirty-two, but his collection of model automobiles numbers close to five hundred.

A beautifully restored 1952 Schwinn Green Phantom.

A few more of the bicycles that are in Bill's bicycle collection, which numbers close to one hundred.

A 1947 Cushman Eagle motor scooter.

A 1950 Schwinn Whizzer, parked next to a 100-year-old solid barbell.

An assortment of bicycles all over 100 years old, sharing space in Bill's office.

An 1896 Colson Model 46 woman's bicycle, equipped with wooden fender, wooden chain guard and wooden rims. Fifty-pound solid dumbbells rest on the floor keeping it company.

Bill's latest acquisition is a rare Land Rower, made in the mid 1980s. (Talk about a ball to ride!) The machine was a gift to Bill from his dear friend Ashrita Furman. (2003)

I SURVIVED THE BARN

In 1976, Judy and I purchased a small ranch in southern Oregon and had the property altered to fit our needs. The ranch is nestled on the edge of hundreds of miles of forest, with only a handful of neighbors to share the beautiful view of the Rogue Valley. The property consists of a Spanish-style home, a guesthouse, a ten-car garage which houses some of our antique car collection, numerous workshops and the most famous building, the "Barn," which is our huge home gym.

For years we lived in the guest house and used the main house like a dorm building for the many friends and aspiring bodybuilders who came to visit, train, and regenerate. As my travel schedule became busier, we moved into the main house and now use the guesthouse for a more select group of family and friends. In all the years we have lived in Oregon, the "Barn" has been open to friends, family and neighbors. Judy and I train six days a week; our workouts have been cut back to 1 1/2 hours each day. My other current training partners, Jim Mess and Bob Autry, are accustomed to the early morning training. Workouts begin at 4:00 a.m. sharp! Saturdays, we often begin at 5:00 a.m. with a few extra guests and "drop-ins," which makes for lots of fun and camaraderie. A few of our visitors have suggested we issue T-shirts proclaiming, "I Survived the Barn." Once the workout is over, you walk out the barn door and breathe deeply of the fresh air and gaze down into the valley, while listening to the birds singing. You just have to smile and be thankful. It's like our little bit of heaven.

Before 4:00 a.m., the sun may not be up yet in rural Oregon, but bodybuilder Pearl is, working out in the red barn he has turned into a gym.

Left: People have come from around the world to train in the "Barn." Illustration by Kurt Schulten.

Left: Dennis Tinerino traveled with Bill giving exhibitions around the world for nearly twenty years before ending up in Bill's "Barn." (1967 AAU Mr. America, 1968 NABBA Amateur Mr. Universe)

Chris Dickerson won the 1982 IFBB Mr. Olympia after spending months in the "Barn." His favorite words before each set of exercise were, "By the Gods!"

Left: Jim Morris, a true friend of Bill and Judy, refuses to start his training at 4:00 a.m. when visiting Bill and Judy in Talent, Oregon. (1973 AAU Mr. America, 1996 IFBB Masters Mr. Olympia)

Right: Joe Distinti not only survived training in the "Barn" while acting as one of Chris Dickerson's training partners for the IFBB Mr. Olympia contest, but also he brought the word "training" to an all new height.

Lynn Conkwright and Chris Dickerson were winners of the International Pairs Competition in 1981. Both spent hours in Bill's "Barn" preparing for the contest.

Right: Billy Knight called the Pearl's guest house his home away from home. (1980/1981 IFBB Mr. Australia)

Donnie Anderson was another who survived the "Barn" and could smile about it.

Diana Dennis didn't take a back seat to anyone in the "Barn." She wasn't satisfied with a workout unless she did at least fifty reps for every exercise.

Photograph taken in the "Barn." Front Row: Rocky Edwards, Chris Dickerson. Second Row: Terry Edwards, Billy Knight, Bill Pearl, Brad Krayer. Third Row: Joe Distinti.

To Bill & Judy
Thanks for all
for all your
help &
encouragement
Clarence
Aug-198

Leona Dunn was a regular at the "Barn" for years. She placed well in her weight class when she competed in the 1987 AAU Miss America contest.

With one workout in the "Barn," Bill got Clarence Bass hooked on early morning training.

The Heathcote family from Bolton, England, came for a visit. Ken insisted on running 20 miles a day, including Sundays.

Don Farnsworth trained with Bill in the 1950s while in the Navy. Fifty years later Don won the "Over-Sixty" division of the "Bill Pearl Classic." They have remained the best of friends and Don trains in the "Barn" whenever he gets the opportunity.

Beth Lopez came from Geelong, Australia, to train with the crew in the "Barn."

Albert Mandell of Thor Exercise Tools has trained in the "Barn," but Bill found it was easier to get him to pose for a photograph than to get him up to train at 4:00 a.m.

Left: Christine Charles came from Birmingham, England, for a visit, but left early because she missed her "fish and chips." (1972 NABBA Miss Universe)

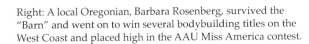

Right: A local Oregonian, Barbara Rosenberg, survived the "Barn" and went on to win several bodybuilding titles on the West Coast and placed high in the AAU Miss America contest.

Left: Another "Barn" group photograph. Kneeling is Sergio Bevilocqua, Canadian Olympian weightlifting champion. Standing behind Sergio is Brad Krayer, Alex Montgomery, former gym owner in Surrey, B.C., Bill Pearl and Rocky Edwards.

Devoted to the Science of Bodybuilding

MUSCULAR DEVELOPMENT®

DECEMBER 1972

75¢
PDC

BUILDING YOUR BASIC
STRUCTURE—THE RIB BOX

TRAIN AT HOME
OR IN A GYM—
WHICH IS BETTER?

HERCULES IN THE FLESH!

SWAYBACK—
A BACK CONDITION
YOU CAN REMEDY

BILL PEARL

Appendix III

THANKS FOR THE MEMORIES

Regardless of the future, the past has been so good that I have very few regrets. My life has been beautiful, thanks to those that I have met along the way. The following pages are dedicated to just a few of these wonderful people through some of the photographs in my collection.

A perfect example of the camaraderie that marked this golden era. A get-together at the home of George and Tuesday Coates in 1994. Seated on couch are Sam Loprinzi, John Grimek, George Coates, Bill Pearl and Vic Boff. Seated on the floor are Joe Abbenda, Dennis Tinerino, Leo Stern, Rosemary Hallum, Joe Marino and Reg Ireland." And a good time was had by all."

Left: "Would I do it all over again? You can bet I would!"

Boyer Coe and Bill in the mid 1970s.

They don't come much bigger, better, or nicer than Lou Ferrigno. He deserves the best that life has to offer.

Vic Boff, head of the Oldetime Barbell and Strongmen Association, congratulates Bill and Leo Stern for being Guests of Honor at the 1994 annual reunion.

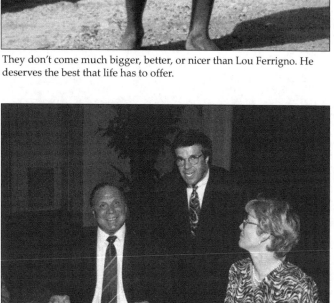

Jay Megna, Executive Vice President of Life Fitness, poses with Judy and Bill at the Life Fitness Awards Banquet, in 2002.

Boyer Coe shakes hands with Ed Corney 25 years after Ed won the IFBB Mr. America and Mr. Universe titles. Photo taken in Las Vegas in 2002.

Massive Paul Dillett and Bill, in 2003.

70-year-old Bill and 80-year-old Bob Delmonteque stop for a photograph, with 85-year-old Jack LaLanne, in 2001.

Massive Anthony Clark, who officially has bench pressed 800 pounds.

John Terpak of the York Barbell Company, Diane Bennett, Bill and Jules Bacon, the oldest living Mr. America winner, pose for a photograph in 1993.

Bill, Angela Grimek and Tuesday and George Coates at the "Old-Timers Get Together" in San Diego, California, in 1991.

Phil Hill, world famous race car driver, and Bill at the Donnington Raceway in central England. Photo taken in the late 1980s.

Bill Kazmaier, one of the strongest of the modern strongmen. He continues to be a positive spokesperson for the sport.

At the Grand Opening of the World's Gym in Calgary, Alberta, Canada, in 2002. Posing with Bill are Henry Caulker, Patrick Neadow and Kevin Harrison.

At the 2002 SWIS Fitness Convention in Toronto, Ontario, Canada. Seated are Winston Roberts and Bill and Lee Haney. Standing are Dr. Ken Kinakin and Scott Abel.

Bill shaking hands with "Cameo" John outside the Coliseum in Rome, in 1967. The box in "Cameo's" hand was filled with semi-precious stones, which he sold to all-comers. He was able to put five of his children through medical school.

Arnold Schwarzenegger jokingly trying to talk Bill out of his 1971 NABBA Professional Mr. Universe trophy.

Ivan Putsky, professional wrestler, breaks bread, rather than bones, with Bill.

Don Farnsworth, Pat Casey, the first to officially bench press 600 pounds, Bill, and Joe Abbenda, former AAU Mr America and NABBA Mr. Universe. Photo taken in 1995.

Sri Chinmoy and Bill in 1998.

Bill and Paul Anderson did an appearance together in Denver, Colorado, during the mid 1960s. Paul's warm-up for his squats was over the world record. He ended up the night by squatting over one thousand pounds.

When Bill has questions about weight-training and wants expert advice, he phones Kate Brill-Daily in Boston, Massachusetts.

Bill working out with long-time friend Raymond Long, at the Personal Best Health Club in Deland, Florida.

Pearl, Ray Schaeffer and Jack Delinger sharing a "spot of tea" in Merry Ole England in 1956. All three were Mr. America and Mr. Universe winners.

John Grimek, Larry Scott and Bill, in 1991.

Isaac Hayes, legendary singer, musician and movie star, shaking hands with Bill during a workout in Atlanta, Georgia, in the 1980s.

George Eiferman, 1948 AAU Mr. America, encouraging Bill as he bends a 70-penny tent spike at the Embassy Auditorium, in Los Angeles, California, in the early 1960s.

Bill and David Young have chalked up hundreds of thousands of miles promoting Life Fitness exercise equipment. David watches over Bill to make sure he does not get lost.

Bob Kennedy, editor of *Muscle Mag International*, has been a strong supporter of Pearl for too many years to remember.

Alan Brunacini, Fire Chief of Phoenix, Arizona, and Bill's training partner at Bill's Sacramento Gym. They still train together when Bill attends the annual Phoenix Fire Department Health and Fitness Training seminars.

Scott Wilson, 1981 N.P.C. Mr. International and another by-product of the San Diego, California, area.

Grimek, Schwarzenegger, Pearl and Goodrich. Each had their own story to tell.

Gunnery Sergeant Sam Griffiths and Bill smile as movie star Audie Murphy, the most highly decorated soldier of World War II, and a U.S. Marine instructor pose for a publicity photo, in the 1960s.

Judy and Bill were guests of Albert Busek in Munich, Germany, in the 1980s. Bill guest-posed at the European Championship.

Albert Busek, publisher of the German magazine *Sport Revue*, honored Bill with a cover for the November 1980 issue.

A rare photograph of two of the all-time legends of bodybuilding, Steve Reeves and Reg Park, in 1952.

Bill shaking Reg Park's hand as Steve Reeves looks on. Photograph taken at the 50th NABBA Mr. Universe contest held in Birmingham, England, in 1998.

"Jab with your left, punch with your right!" That was Bill's boyhood friend Al Simmon's take on life. Photograph taken in 1952.

"Beauty" (right) and the "Beast" (left).

Judy and Bill enjoying a pleasant visit with Benno Dahmen, publisher of *Sport and Fitness* magazine in Krefeld, Germany. Bill appeared on nearly 100 magazine covers during his career.

A rare photograph of four great British bodybuilders in the mid-1950s. Front row: John Isaacs and Buster McShane. Top row: Reg Park and Rubin Martin.

A group of true health advocates. George Eiferman, Armand Tanny, Russ Warner, George Coates, George Redpath and Reg Park, in the 1990s.

Dr. Sal Arria, D.C., ISSA Executive Director

Mike Katz, 1970 IFBB Mr. America, gives Bill a warm smile and big hug during the celebration of Sri Chinmoy's 14th Weightlifting Anniversary, in 1999.

Samir Bannout, 1983 IFBB Mr. Olympia, had good reason to look so happy. With his physique, why wouldn't he smile!

Mike Uretz, Bill and Mike Katz pay respect to Ed Guiliani at the World's Gym 2002 annual convention.

Red Lerille, 1960 AAU Mr. America, has a larger collection of toys than Bill. His hobbies range from vintage airplanes to cars, bicycles, motorcycles and everything in between.

Cory Everson set a standard of professionalism so high for women's bodybuilding, it has been nearly impossible for others to meet.

Frank Zane beat the best! If he was on stage, he would be in the best possible condition.

John Grimek (left) "holding court" in the parking lot of the Pasadena Health Club, while Charlie Moss, M.D., Bill, Jim Morris and Christopher Solow pay strict attention. Photo taken in the 1970s.

Five AAU Mr. America winners: Bert Goodrich 1939, John Grimek 1940-1941, Jules Bacon 1943, Bill Pearl 1953 and Joe Abbenda 1962.

John Davis, Olympic and world champion weightlifter, was a big inspiration to Bill. Bill stated, "John was a class act."

The degree of development of the new age bodybuilders, such as Lee Priest, is nearly beyond Bill's comprehension.

George Eiferman, former AAU Mr. America and Peter Lupis, from Mission Impossible, congratulate Bill for being entered into the Joe Weider Hall of Fame, in 1994.

Len Sell, 1962 NABBA Professional Mr. Universe is still in remarkable condition and continues to operate a successful health club in England.

235

Jim Flanagan, one of the original Nautilus gang from the 1970s, who has continued to make his mark in the fitness industry.

George Koeck in the early 1960s. George still works as a forester for the State of New Jersey.

Bill, Ronnie Coleman, Pat O'Dell, and Greg Bahnfleth, at the grand opening of the new 56,000- square-foot fitness facility at the Quantico, Virginia, U.S. Marine base, in 2003.

Bill and Judy continually thank Chris and Beth Clawson, of Life Fitness, for their kindness and support over the years.

Joe Abbenda was the by-product of a one-car garage home gym in Queens, New York. He won the 1962 AAU Mr. America and the 1962 NABBA Amateur Mr. Universe, as well as the 1963 NABBA Professional Mr. Universe.

Ted Baker, formerly with Universal Gym Equipment. Ted has been an inspiration to Bill and a friend for nearly forty years. He still plays hard-core hockey and is someone you would want on your side in a dark alley on a dark night.

Kevin Grodski, Life Fitness President and CEO, continues to keep Bill busy and is always willing to listen to Pearl's odd-ball comments and theories.

Appendix IV

THE GOLDEN AGE OF STRENGTH TRAINING

Over the past five decades I've traveled the world over, teaching the benefits and history of resistance weight training and bodybuilding. The following pages are a brief summary of this history, dating back thousands of years. The material has come from boxes of memorabilia that has been helpful to my fifty-plus years of physical culture research.

I would now like to take you on a pictorial journey through the Golden Age of Strength Training. This brief summary is being conducted through my eyes and the associations that have influenced me over my lifetime.

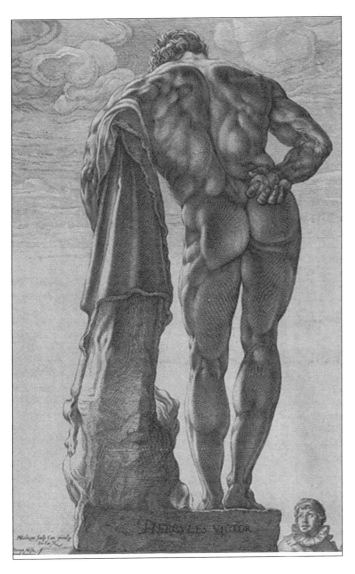

Before we begin this journey, let's back up not one hundred years or even two hundred years but two thousand years! The first advanced system of weight training originated with the ancient Greeks. Unlike today's warfare, which is based on highly developed technology, then victory was dependent on the physical capabilities and skills of the warriors. The word "gymnasium" stems from the Greek word "gymnazein." In translation, it means to train naked, which is what ancient athletes and warriors usually did two thousand years ago.

Left: Bill quotes, "Perhaps the earliest record in existence of any form of resistance exercise is a drawing on the walls of a funerary chapel in Beni-Hassan in Egypt. The drawing was made approximately 4,500 years ago."

Two hundred years ago, the person most responsible for popularizing physical culture to a limited number on the European continent was Friederick Jahn. In 1812, Jahn began a gymnastic organization, calling his centers Turnvereins. His gymnastic society became so popular that immigrants migrating to the United States in the mid-1850s formed Turnvereins in St. Louis, Philadelphia, Boston and New York. This played an important role in early American physical culture.

Hippolyte Triat (a gypsy born in Spain in the early 1800s), built a magnificent health club, the "Gymnase Triat", in Paris, France, in 1847.

Hippolyte Triat's club was years ahead of its time and nothing this elaborate was to be seen in the United States for another three-quarters of a century.

By the turn of the 19th century, health clubs were opening in several of the major metropolitan areas throughout the more progressive countries in Europe, such as France, England and Germany. The clubs featured most everything that was athletically popular: boxing, wrestling, track and field, aerobics and weight training. All of these activities are still popular today.

One of the first commercial health clubs in the United States opened its doors in 1875. The club was the YMCA in Boston, Massachusetts. Though the European gyms far surpassed the YMCA with regard to exercise equipment, what made this facility so unique was that it featured showers and dressing rooms.

The individual most responsible for bringing physical culture to the forefront, in Europe and America, during the late 19th and early 20th century was Friederick Muller, better known by his stage name Eugen Sandow. Standing 5′ 9″ tall and weighing 190 pounds, Sandow began his professional career at the age of 18, as a wrestler and strongman. Many considered him one of the strongest men in the world. Prior to coming to the United States in 1893, he performed in most major theaters throughout Europe, where he competed against such worthy opponents as Cyclops, Apollo and the Saxon Brothers, as well as many others.

Sandow met Florenz Ziegfeld at the Chicago world's fair in 1893. He assisted in the judging of the first physique contest held in the United States. He also gave a posing exhibition in addition to performing some amazing feats of strength. Ziegfeld was so impressed that he signed Sandow to a long-term contact with the Ziegfeld Follies, reportedly paying him $3,500.00 per week.

Sandow became an instant star throughout America. His name appeared on most everything masculine: Sandow Cigars, Sandow Cigarettes and Sandow Chewing Tobacco. Nearly every tonsorial parlor (barber shop) in the country had a photograph of Sandow hanging from its wall to promote the sale of moustache wax.

Louis Cyr at Sohmer Park, Montreal, 1891

Sandow's major rival on the North American continent was the magnificent Louis Cyr, born in 1863 near Montreal, Quebec, Canada. Some historians have suggested that Cyr was the strongest man that ever lived. At the age of 18, he stood 5′ 10″ tall and weighed 295 pounds. He is credited with a 535-pound one-finger lift, a one-hand lift of 987 pounds and a back lift of 4,300 pounds, which is a record that stood for fifty years.

Louis Attila (Louis Durlacher) established the first private health club in the United States in 1894, in New York City. Prior to coming to America from Germany, Attila was the tutor of noted physical culturists, kings and queens. Louis Attila also assisted the younger Eugen Sandow by often acting as his manager.

Siegmund Klein was born on April 10, 1902 in Thorn, West Prussia, Germany. He moved to Cleveland, Ohio, with his parents in 1903. Siegmund took over the daily operation of Attila's gym in 1924, after Louis Attila's death, and married Grace, Louis Attila's daughter, three years later. He ran the club six days a week, twelve hours a day, for the next sixty years. It was there that I met many of the old-time strongmen that I admired and read about as a youngster.

Photographs taken in the early 1970s of Siegmund Klein's health club. Much of the equipment was still the same as when Klein's father-in-law, Louis Attila, established the club in 1894.

Muscular Young Men after the Medal

THE NATIONAL POLICE GAZETTE

THE LEADING ILLUSTRATED SPORTING JOURNAL IN THE WORLD.

Copyrighted for 1902 by the Proprietor, RICHARD K. FOX, The Fox Building, Franklin Square Publishing, Printing and Engraving House, New York City.

RICHARD K. FOX, Editor and Publisher.

NEW YORK SATURDAY, JULY 19, 1902.

The *National Police Gazette*, established in 1895, became one of the first major publications to promote physical culture in the United States. The *National Police Gazette* was selling over two-and-a-quarter million copies each week, at a time when the population of the United States was only sixty-four million. The pink-paged periodical concentrated on physical activities and sports, while covering the crimes, scandals and passions of that era. Josephine Blatt (Minerva), (below left) the world's strongest woman, Tony Massimo (below right), Cyr, Sandow, Attila, and others were regularly featured.

The *National Police Gazette* sponsored a photo physique contest by mail in 1902. Thousands of entries were received. An indicator of the quality of physiques at that time is the fact that the young man pictured did not qualify for a trophy.

In the early 1900s, the Global Barbell, produced by Louis Attila, was considered one of the finest pieces of exercise equipment money could buy. Drain plugs were inserted into each of the globes, into which sand, shot, lead or water could be added, or removed, to change the weight of the bar. Prior to Attila's innovation, barbells and dumbbells were cast for a fixed poundage.

Alan Calvert, of Canada, designed the Milo Barbell in 1902. With the Milo barbell, assorted weight-plates were placed on the bar inside the globes. For the first time in weight training history, there was now a rather convenient method to increase or decrease the weight of the bar.

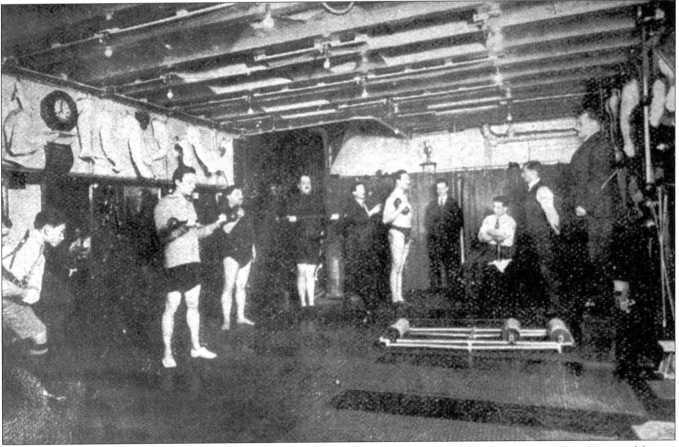

During World War 1 (1914 to 1918), physical culture nearly ground to a halt. Once the hostilities ended, private gyms sprang up in many of the larger cities on the East Coast of the United States.

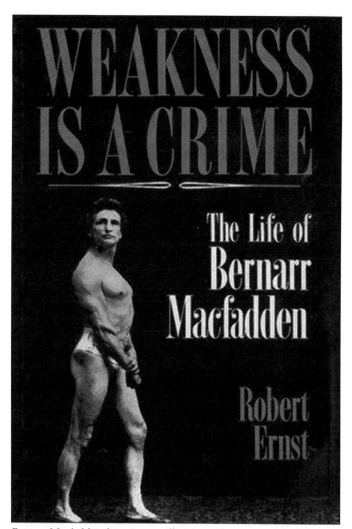

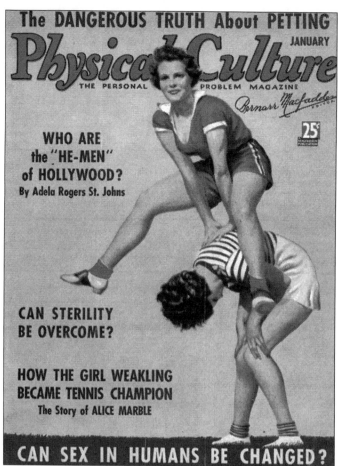

Bernarr Macfadden, born in a small town in Missouri in 1868, was now known as the "Father of Physical Culture." He became the greatest promoter of health foods, exercise, walking and pure water that our country has seen during the past one hundred years. He lived by the slogan "Weakness is a Crime... Don't be a Criminal." This slogan led to the publication of the magazine *Physical Culture,* which Macfadden first published in 1899 and which survived until 1955.

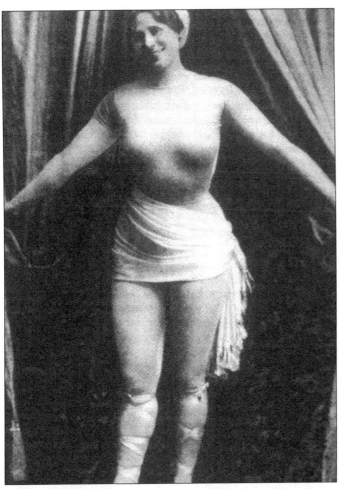

Macfadden sponsored beauty and physique contests for women and men throughout the world, and then featured the winners in *Physical Culture*. He met and married Mary Williamson (top left), in the early 1920s, after she had won his beauty contest in England. Through the pages of *Physical Culture*, she became the epitome of femininity for women worldwide. It is interesting to notice the changes in women's figures from Mary Williamson in the 1920s... to Vera Christensen in the 1950s... and to date, Shirley Green.

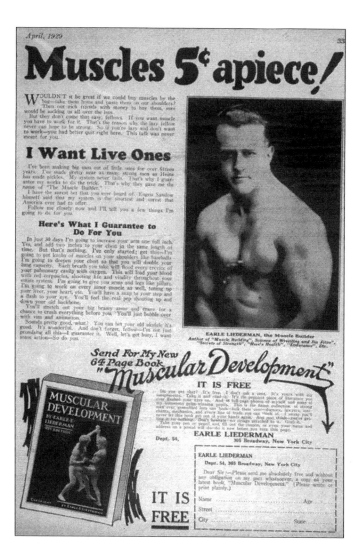

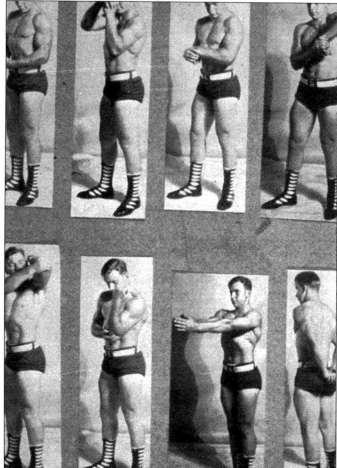

Earle Liederman was so successful at designing a mail order training course series during the 1920s that he became a multi-millionaire. His home-based method of training was to resist one muscle group against another. The advanced training courses required a training partner to apply the resistance. When the stock market crashed in 1929, Liederman lost everything. His mail order business, which was housed in a five-story building in downtown Manhattan, New York, was liquidated, causing over 300 employees to lose their jobs.

Liederman never recovered from his losses. He wrote several books on weight training, which are now collector's items. By 1968, he had survived thirty-two cancer operations, but on the way to the hospital for number thirty-three, he was killed in an auto accident.

Angelo Siciliano, better known to the world as Charles Atlas, stood as America's symbol of manhood and virility for nearly fifty years. It was winning a photo physique contest sponsored by Macfadden that began Atlas's journey to prominence. In 1924, he began a mail order course promoting physique development that was similar to Earle Liederman's. His system of training was called, "Dynamic Tension," and claimed that a person became "muscle bound" by lifting weights. Atlas died in 1972. That year alone, over 23,000 of his fitness courses were sold worldwide.

Bob Hoffman (above left, wearing hat) founded the York Barbell Company in 1938. Through the pages of *Strength & Health* magazine, he advertised an adjustable weight set for $22.95. The York Big Ten Special made it affordable for practically every household in America to improve their health and fitness through weight training. My first weight set was the York Big Ten Special. I ordered the set at the end of 1941 and took delivery in 1945, due to World War II rationing of materials. I was positive the weight set would transform me from the "before" photograph to the "after" photograph in the few short months the magazine promised.

An evolution of *Iron Man* magazine over a sixty-year period. Originally published in 1936 in Alliance, Nebraska, by Peary and Mabel Rader, *Iron Man* was the kind of magazine that hard-core bodybuilders and weightlifters would choose if they could only afford a single subscription. The sole purpose of the magazine was to cover the sport of weightlifting and bodybuilding. The editorial pages were open to any qualified writer.

"Vic" Tanny's Gym
1417-A SECOND STREET
Santa Monica, California

LARGEST AND BEST EQUIPPED
BARBELL GYM IN THE WEST

Body Building	RATES	
and	3 months . $12.0	
	6 months . 20.0	
Reducing	1 year . . 35.0	

Vic Tanny opened the first private health club on the West Coast of the United States in 1939. The gym was located in Santa Monica, California. In 1943, while traveling with my father to Arizona, we stopped at the club. I carried the business card Tanny gave me in my wallet for the next twenty-five years, hoping that one day I could take advantage of his membership rates.

By the early 1950s, Joe Weider's magazine *Your Physique*, first published in 1940, had a readership large enough to compete with Bob Hoffman's *Strength & Health*. The rivalry between the two publications was unbelievable. Weider hired Reg Park and Clancy Ross, hoping to steal some of the thunder from John Grimek, who worked for Hoffman. In retrospect, Grimek had no rivals. His physique was years ahead of its time.

By the late 1940s, the West Coast of the United States had become the Mecca for bodybuilding. The largest draw was Muscle Beach, located in Santa Monica, California. This small stretch of sand attracted the best male and female bodies of the day, including Harold Zinkin, Jack LaLanne, John Grimek, Joe Gold, Vic Tanny, Siegmund Klein, Pudgy Stockton, Barbara Thomason and Beverly Jocker. Every weekend thousands of people spent hours watching some of the greatest gymnasts, bodybuilders and weightlifters performing feats practically unheard of. The photograph to the left is of Grimek, Zinkin and Klein in California, in 1949.

257

Steve Reeves (above), AAU Mr. America, NABBA Mr. Universe and famous movie star, was "King of Muscle Beach." Other legends were Chuck Ahrens (below left), the 300-pound strongman. Paul Anderson (below center) can be seen at the beach clowning around with the girls. Beverly Jocker (below right) was crowned the 1952 Miss Muscle Beach, and was then considered the epitome of femininity.

During the early 1950s health clubs began springing up all along the West Coast of the United States in cities with a population of around 100,000. Most of the facilities were less than 5,000 square-feet and filled with makeshift equipment. There were no parking lots or air conditioning. An example of the equipment I was so proud of was our lat pull-down machine. To perform the movement, I installed two pulleys to the ceiling, ran a cable to a metal basket and a curved bar, and then sat on a block of wood.

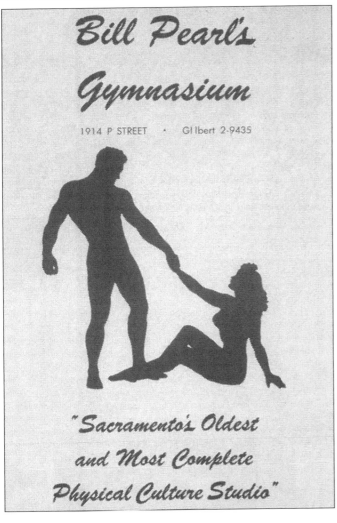

As later as the 1950s, in order for physique contests to draw large crowds, they took on a variety show format. The poster for the Ed Yarick Show of 1954, held in Oakland, California, featured fourteen acts with former heavyweight boxing champion Max Baer acting as Master of Ceremonies. The curtains opened with my posing routine and closed with Grimek's exhibition of posing and muscle control. The best seat in the theater sold for $2.40.

Around the same time, the fitness industry received a giant boost when Jack LaLanne moved his morning television fitness show from San Francisco to Los Angeles, California. Nearly every housewife in America who was exposed to a television set began each morning by training with Jack.

It seemed that all the top bodybuilders of the 1950s were becoming movie stars: Steve Reeves (above), Reg Park (left), Micky Hargitay, Lou Degni, Reg Lewis, Dominic Juliano, Armand Tanny, Zabo Kozewski, Seymour Koenig and Joe Gold to mention a few.

Leo Stern and I began a mail order business in the mid-1960s similar to that of the old-time strongmen. We produced and sold training courses, health foods, posing trunks and form-fitting T-shirts. It wasn't long before other top physique stars began emulating what we were doing.

Stern went so far as to import Russian Olympic weightlifting sets into the United States. Pat Casey, the first person to officially bench press over 600 pounds, is seen demonstrating the Russian set. Notice the flimsy bench that Pat was using for such a heavy lift. He weighed over 300 pounds; plus there was close to 352 pounds on the bar. Everything was held together by the small nut and bolt at the base of the bench!

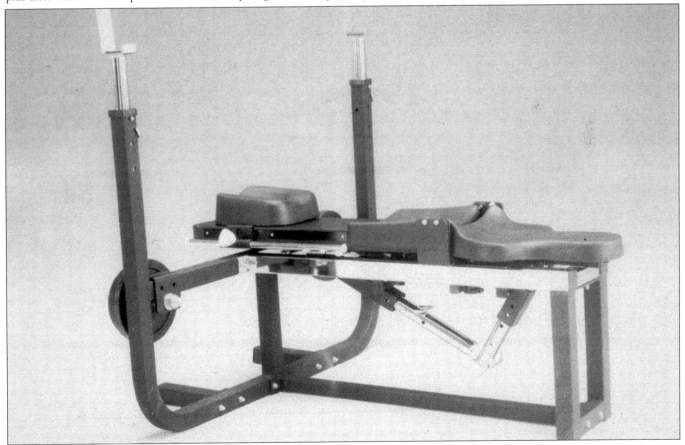

At the same time, I attempted to design the ultimate piece of exercise equipment. I patented a series of exercise benches that contoured to the users body. The idea was to have more overall body support while doing an exercise.

Rachel McLish took over where Lisa Lyon left off. Her bodybuilding career lasted four years, which included winning the IFBB Miss Olympia contest in 1980 and again in 1982. She remained one of the best spokespersons for female bodybuilding years after her retirement from competition.

Lisa Lyon brought women into the sport of competitive bodybuilding by winning the first World Women's Bodybuilding Championships in 1979.

By 1984 Lee Haney began his domination of the sport of men's competitive bodybuilding. His domination lasted for the next ten years. Lee was as nice as he was big and is still active in the sport, encouraging others to become their best.

Bill Kazmaier was crowned the World's Strongest Man, in the mid 1980s. There were few feats of strength, regardless of who specializes in them, that Kazmaier couldn't either duplicate or outdo.

Cory Everson added an all-new dimension to women's bodybuilding with her professional approach. She won the IFBB Miss Olympia title six times from 1984 to 1989. Both she and Rachel McLish attempted to keep femininity alive in the sport.

Bev Francis, another top Miss Olympia competitor, decided upon a different approach.

Dorian Yates, from Birmingham, England, dominated the sport of bodybuilding until the late 1990s. Dorian was a no-nonsense bodybuilder who took his weight training extremely seriously. I predicted injuries would run him out of the sport. He trained so heavily, eventually something had to go.

Ronnie Coleman won his first Mr. Olympia title in 1999. At a height of 5' 11" his contest weight is 280 pounds. He won the overall title, Mr. Texas, at his first bodybuilding contest in 1990, and the rest, as they say, is history.

Yet, with all of the changes over the last one hundred years of the fitness industry, how much has really changed? Here is a comparison between the most modern equipment on the market today and the ultra-modern equipment of 1903.

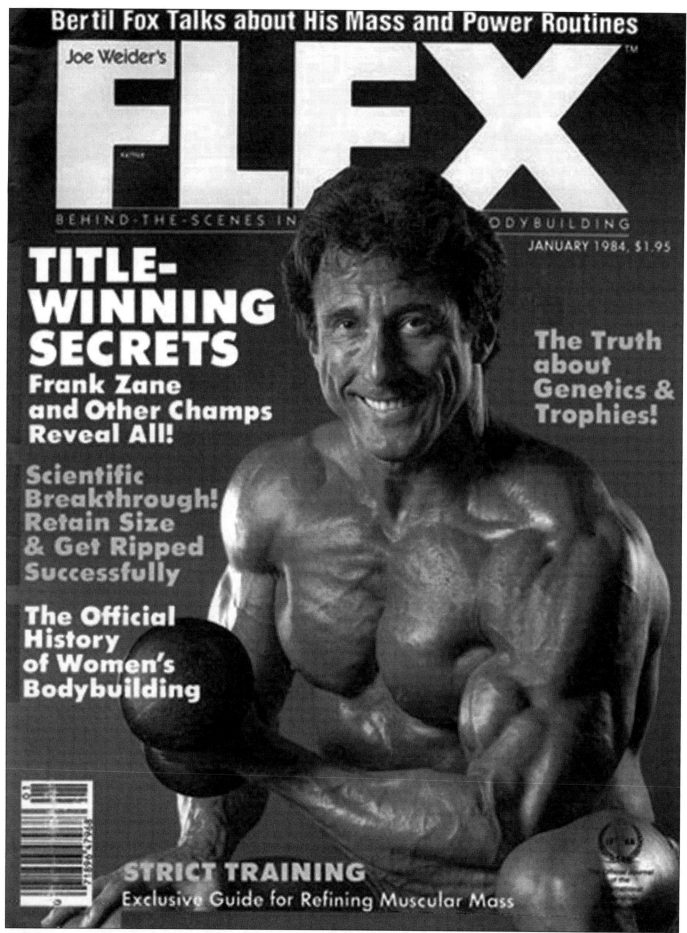

Bertil Fox Talks about His Mass and Power Routines

Joe Weider's

FLEX™

BEHIND·THE·SCENES IN ━━ ODYBUILDING

JANUARY 1984, $1.95

TITLE-WINNING SECRETS
Frank Zane and Other Champs Reveal All!

The Truth about Genetics & Trophies!

Scientific Breakthrough! Retain Size & Get Ripped Successfully

The Official History of Women's Bodybuilding

STRICT TRAINING
Exclusive Guide for Refining Muscular Mass

In closing, we see Frank Zane, one of the greatest modern-day bodybuilders, featured on the cover of a major fitness magazine, doing a concentrated-biceps curl with a cast-iron dumbbell that may have been in existence for well over one hundred years.

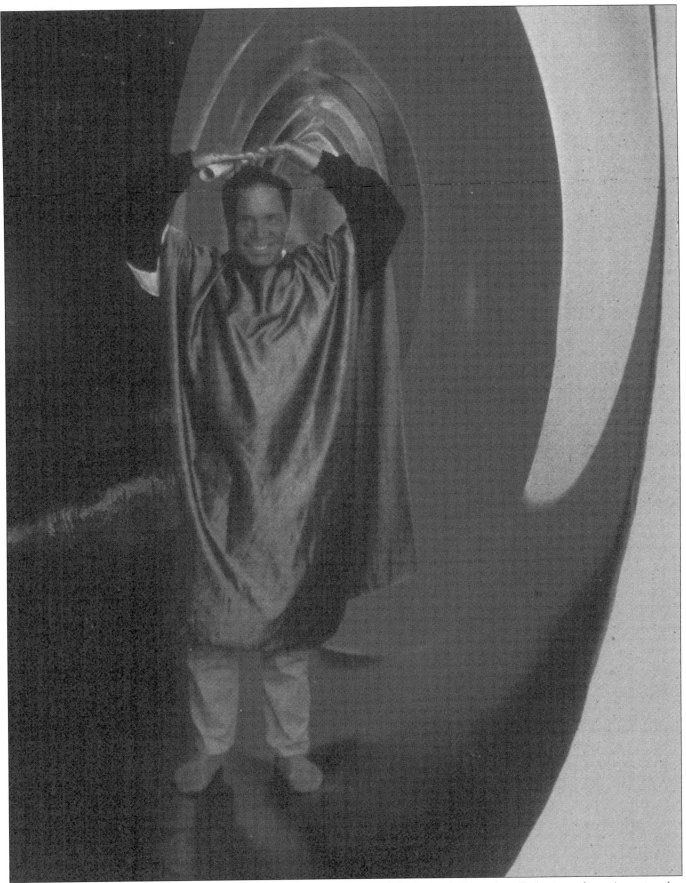

Therefore, in my opinion, the major change in the fitness industry over the past hundreds of years has not been the business, the equipment, or the techniques on how to become fit. The change within the past hundreds of years in the fitness industry has been, and will always be, the faces of the people. Those that are shown in this book will come and go and be replaced with new ones. Perhaps your face is next in the distinguished line of legends.

Bill Pearl

BIBLIOGRAPHY

Bass, Clarence. *Ripped 3: The Recipes, The Routines and The Reasons*. Albuquerque, New Mexico: Clarence Bass Ripped Enterprises, 1986.

Beecroft, John. *Kipling - A selection of His Stories and Poems Volume II*. Garden City, New York: Doubleday & Co, Inc., 1892-1956.

Chapman, David L. *Sandow the Magnificent*. Illinois: University of Illinois Press, 1994.

Darden, Ellington, Ph.D., *The Nautilus Bodybuilding Book*. Chicago, Illinois: Contemporary Books, Inc., 1982.

Draper, Dave. *Brother Iron Sister Steel*. Aptos, California: On Target Publications, 2001.

Ernst, Robert. *Weakness Is A Crime*, Garden City, New York: Syracuse University Press, 1991.

Fair, John D. *Muscletown U.S.A.* University Park, Pennsylvania: The Pennsylvania State University Press, 1999.

Ferrigno, Lou. *Lou Ferrigno's Guide to Personal Power, Bodybuilding and Fitness for Everyone.*:, 1994.

Felleman, Hazel. *The Best Loved Poems of the American People.*Garden City, New York: Doubleday and Compnay, Inc., 1936.

George, David L. *The Family Book of Best Loved Poems*. Garden City, New York: Doubleday and Company, Inc., 1952.

Haney, Lee. *Totalee Awesome*, Atlanta, Georgia: Peachtree Publishers, LTD. 1987.

Ironman Magazine and Peter Sisco. *Ironman's Ultimate Guide to Building Muscle Mass*. Chicago, Illinois: Contemporary Books, 2000.

Ironman Magazine; Peter Sisco. *Ironman's Ultimate Body Building Encyclopedia*. Chicago, Illinois: Contemporary Books, 1999.

Kennedy, Robert. *Beef It: Upping the Muscle Mass*. New York, New York: Sterling Publishing Co., Inc., 1983.

Kennedy, Robert. *Hardcore Bodybuilding: The Blood, Sweat and Tears of Pumping Iron*. New York, New York: Sterling Publishing Co., Inc., 1982.

Kennedy, Robert. *Muscleblasting; Brief and Brutal Shock Training*, New York: Sterling Publishing Co., Inc., 1988.

Kennedy, Robert; Weis, Dennis B. *New Scientific Bodybuilding Secrets*. Chicago, Illinois: Contemporary Books, Inc. 1986.

Kennedy, Robert; Weis, Dennis B. *Raw Muscle! New Hardcore Technique for Superhuman Strength and Muscle Mass!*. Chicago, Illinois: Contemporary Books, Inc. 1989.

LeClaire, Chris. *Steve Reeves: World's to Conquer*. Rockland, Massachusetts: Monomoy Books. 1999.

Lyon, Jack M.; Gundry, Linda Ririe; Parry, Jay A.; Jensen, Devan. *Poems That Lift The Soul*. Salt Lake City, Utah: Deseret Book Company, 1998.

Pearl, Bill. *Key's to the Inner Universe*. Phoenix, Oregon: Bill Pearl Enterprises, Inc., 2000.

Pearl, Bill. *Getting Stronger 2nd Edition*. Bolinas, California: Shelter Publications, Inc., 2001.

Spielman, Ed. *The Mighty Atom: The Life and Times of Joseph L. Greenstein*. New York, New York: The Viking Press, 1979.

Spraque, Ken; Reynolds, Bill. *The Gold's Gym Book of Bodybuilding*. Chicago, Illinois: Contemporary Books, 1983.

Strossen, Randall J. *Paul Anderson: The Mightiest Minister.* Nevada City, California: IronMind Enterprises, Inc., 1999.

Ward, Robert Dr.; Ward, Paul Dr. *Encylopedia of Weight-Training.* Laguna Hills, California: QPT Publications, 1991.

Webster, David. *Sons of Samson: Volume 1.* Irvine, Scotland: DP Webster, 1993.

Webster, David. *Barbells and Beefcake: An Illustrated Story of Bodybuilding.* Irvine, Scotland: DP Webster, 1979.

Weider, Joe. Mr. Olympia: *The History of Bodybuilding's Greatest Contest.* New York, New York: St. Martin's Press, 1983.

Zinkin, Harold; Hearn Bonnie. *Remembering Muscle Beach.* Santa Monica, California: Angel City Press, 1999.

PHOTO CREDITS

Joe Abbenda
Scott Abel
Chuck Ahrens
Paul Anderson
Gregor Arax
Charles Atlas (Angelo Siciliano)
Jules Bacon
John Balik
Samir Bannout
Dr. Jack Barnathan
Clarence Bass
Diane Bennett
Reneé Pearl Bernard
Doug Brignole
George Bruce
Don Burns
Albert Busek
Jimmy Caruso
Pat Casey
Sri Chinmoy
Anthony Clark
George Coates
Boyer Coe
Ronnie Coleman
Lynn Conkwright
Ed Corney
Louis Cyr
John Davis
Bob Delmontique
Monique Delmontique
Chris Dickerson
Paul Dillet
Dave Draper
Dick DuBois
George Eiferman
Cory Everson
Robert Ernst
Christy Farnsworth
Don Farnsworth
Lou Ferrigno
Ashrita Furman
Life Fitness
Bev Francis
Ken Germano
John Paul Getty
David Chapman
Vince Gironda
Joe Gold
Bert Goodrich
Paul Grant
Shirley Green
Angela Grimek
John Grimek
Ed Guiliani

Lee Guthery
Lee Haney
Richard Hadder
Isaac Hayes
Oscar Heidenstam
Ron Hemelgarn
Bob Hoffman
Rockwell International
Cameo John
Dave Johns
Arthur Jones
Jerry Kahn
Mike Katz
Bill Kazmaier
Breigh Kelley
Bob Kennedy
Dr. Ken Kinakin
Abakash Konopiaty
Tommy Kono
Sandy Koufax
Steve Kilisanin
Zabo Koszewski
Billy Knight
Jack LaLanne
Earl Liederman
Dallas Long, M.D.,
Raymond Long
Chris Lund
Lisa Lyon
Ian MacQueen
Mohamed Makkawy
Earl Maynard
John McCarthy
Rachel McLish
Jay Megna
Mike Mentzer
Jim Morris
Charles (Charlie) Moss, M.D.,
Gene Mozee
Audey Murphy
Augie Nieto
Sergio Oliva
George Paine
Reg Park
Harold F. Pearl
Harold G. Pearl
Judy Pearl
Mildred Pearl
Lee Priest
Ivan Putsky
Mabel Rader
Peary Rader
Steve Reeves
Bill Reynolds

Winston Roberts
Jimmy Robinson
Clarence (Clancy) Ross
Ray Routledge
Fontelle Pearl Salzman
Eugen Sandow (Friederick Muller)
Arnold Schwarzenegger
Elton Sewell
Larry Scott
Al Simmons
Chuck Sipes
Christopher Solow
Leo Stern
Bettye Stern
Pudgy Stockton
Ray Stoddard
Cliff Swanagan
Armand Tanny
Larry Taylor
John Terpak
Barbara Thompson
Dennis Tinerino
Mike Uretz
Ken Waller
Russ Warner
Dave Webster
Ben Weider
Betty Weider
Joe Weider
Steve Weinberg
Doug White
Craig Whitehead, M.D.,
Millard Williamson
Ray Wilson
Kimberly Pearl Wyniarczuk
Dorian Yates
Dave Young
Frank Zane
Vic Zanotti
Art Zeller
Harold Zinkin

This page has been intentionally left blank.

INDEX

This page has been intentionally left blank.